"Language Arts in Action is a book that skillfully blends language arts and media literacy concepts together in a way that makes it possible for every secondary English teacher to engage with adolescent learners and their complex media environments. This book revolutionizes and reinvigorates journalism education at a time when it's never been more important to untangle the blurring boundaries between information, persuasion, and entertainment."

—**Renee Hobbs**, professor of communication studies and director, Media Education Lab, Harrington School of Communication and Media, University of Rhode Island

"A welcome new approach to information literacy, this work utilizes active learning while never losing sight of the activities' connection to larger goals around trust, community engagement, skill development, and how such activities might make for better consumers of news content. This last part is particularly important; active approaches tend to disregard the ultimate impact of such activities on the student as reader and viewer, instead becoming hyper-focused on technical production and polish. *Language Arts in Action*, however, stays centered with activities that will help students think through the nature of capturing and conveying expertise—lessons that readers themselves will likely find useful as well."

—**Mike Caulfield**, research scientist at the University of Washington's Center for an Informed Public and creator of the SIFT methodology for student fact-checking

"A great read for those interested in creating authentic learning experiences for students! *Language Arts in Action* presents a powerful, honest, and moving process of an innovative education model."

—**Yong Zhao**, Foundation Distinguished Professor, School of Education and Human Sciences, University of Kansas and professor in educational leadership, Melbourne Graduate School of Education, University of Melbourne

"If you're committed to breathing new life into language arts teaching, then look no further. This book offers an action-oriented framework that can help you transform ELA teaching into more engaging and meaningful experiences—empowering students to become the authors of their own learning and contributors to their own futures."

—**Ronald A. Beghetto**, Pinnacle West Presidential Chair and professor, Arizona State University

LANGUAGE ARTS IN ACTION

NORTON BOOKS IN EDUCATION

LANGUAGE ARTS in ACTION

Engaging Secondary Students with Journalistic Strategies

Ed Madison
Melissa Wantz
Rachel Guldin

Norton Professional Books

An Imprint of W. W. Norton & Company
Celebrating a Century of Independent Publishing

Note to Readers: Models and/or techniques described in this volume are illustrative or are included for general informational purposes only; neither the publisher nor the author(s) can guarantee the efficacy or appropriateness of any particular recommendation in every circumstance. As of press time, the URLs displayed in this book link or refer to existing sites. The publisher and author are not responsible for any content that appears on third-party websites.

For information about permission to reproduce selections from this book, write to Permissions, W. W. Norton & Company, Inc., 500 Fifth Avenue, New York, NY 10110

For information about special discounts for bulk purchases, please contact W. W. Norton Special Sales at specialsales@wwnorton.com or 800-233-4830

Manufacturing by P.A. Hutchison Company
Production manager: Gwen Cullen

ISBN: 978-1-324-03062-1 (pbk)

W. W. Norton & Company, Inc., 500 Fifth Avenue, New York, NY 10110
www.wwnorton.com

W. W. Norton & Company Ltd., 15 Carlisle Street, London W1D 3BS

1 2 3 4 5 6 7 8 9 0

CONTENTS

ACKNOWLEDGMENTS

The authors wish to acknowledge our editor Carol Collins for believing in this work. Ed Madison would like to acknowledge the Journalistic Learning Initiative's (JLI) distinguished benefactors, Dave and Nancy Petrone, the Roundhouse Foundation, Bi-Mart, and the NewSchools Venture Fund. Also, his family and the many mentors, colleagues, friends, and teachers who have fueled his growth, including Esther Wojcicki, Paul Kandell, Tara Guber, Ritch Colbert, Bob Loudin, Hilary Schacter, Jane Caper, John Goldhammer, Bob Shanks, Woody Fraser, Marianne Williamson, Ray Blanchard, Brian Obie, Sandy Trahan, Brad Kleiner, Ross Anderson, Tracy Bousselot, Matt Coleman, Paul Roth, Renee Hobbs, Tim Gleason, Juan-Carlos Molleda, Julianne Newton, Leslie Steeves, Deb Morrison, Kim Sheehan, and Janet Wasko. Also, the JLI board and team, with special thanks to Glenda Gordon, Hans Boyle, Maya Lazaro, Auna Calipano, Jael Calloway, Jordan Bentz, Jordan Tichenor, Riley Stevenson, Hailey O'Donnell, Noeme Teofilo, and Clarence Kim Dulin.

Melissa Wantz would like to acknowledge the K–12 colleagues who inspired or supported her desire to take risks in the field, especially Dani Bayer, Joe Bova, Lorelle Dawes, Darcy Duffy, Cherie Eulau, April Golden, Ethan Gray, Josiah Guzik, Matt Haines, Robin Houlahan, Yiu Hung Li, Kurt Miller, Margarita Mosqueda, Dan Nelson, Fawn Nguyen, Cindy Nofziger, the late Chris Prewitt, John Puglisi, Edmund J. Sullivan, Kathy Waters, and Kathy Zwiebel. And to the educators in her family—husband Steve Wantz, daughter Megan Larson, son-in-law Tyler Larson, sister Carolyn Bernal, and mom Sue Eastman—you are her heart's teachers.

Rachel Guldin acknowledges those who've supported and informed her work and growth, including her professors, mentors, and classmates in the School of Journalism and Communication at the University of Oregon; her colleagues at Denison University; the community of media scholars and media literacy experts she's met online and at Penn State University, the Union for Democratic Communications, and the Critical Media Literacy Conference of the Americas; and her friends and family, Mom, Dad, Joanna, Becky, John, Sam, and Will.

FOREWORD

I first met University of Oregon professor Ed Madison back in 2010. He was not yet a professor; in fact, he had been a producer for CNN and the CBS Morning Program for years. Now he was searching for a new opportunity.

We were not planning on meeting, but we both ended up in a lecture series sponsored by the Stanford Communication and Media Department. He remembers going there to explore, see who he could meet, and what he would learn. I remember pulling some of my students out of their seventh period advanced journalism class to take them to what was a stimulating discussion about current events.

I don't remember the topic, but I do remember clearly that my students challenged the speaker with their questions. They were not shy, in fact just the opposite, but they were respectful. The students had no fear of asking the questions that others wish they had the courage to ask. At the end of the presentation, when everyone was dispersing, Ed Madison came up to me, wanting to meet these students. He didn't realize they were high school students. He was blown away by their questions and composure. He wanted to know more. He invited me to have an early dinner with him and I readily accepted.

At the dinner, I described the journalism program that these kids were in—and the other 80 kids who were also in my class, but were not at the Stanford event. Intrigued, he wanted to come visit, and I invited him. A few months later, Ed decided to write his doctoral dissertation on my journalism program. That was the beginning of a long, productive collaboration. Ed spent many months observing and documenting the classes. It was a gift for me to have Ed and his insights every day, asking questions and sharing his observations. We focused on how journalism can dramatically improve students' engagement, their critical thinking and writing skills, and even their mental health. Ed and I cocreated the Journalistic Learning Initiative at the University of Oregon in 2015, and Ed then went on to develop the highly successful Effective Communicators Program upon which this book is based.

Ed and his coauthors have brought together in *Language Arts in Action* the many ways in which teaching journalistic techniques can empower kids and hone their skills in civic engagement, collaboration, critical thinking, and communication. These are essential skills for the 21st century that all students should have. The book is packed with examples and suggestions that will be valuable to all teachers, and especially to teachers of English and social studies. The fact that students are allowed so much agency as young journalists fosters and encourages a sense of self-confidence that is rarely seen in teenagers. That confidence carries over to their other classes, and into their adult lives. What teacher would want to miss that opportunity?

Language Arts in Action is an important book on an important topic. The model of instruction explained in the following chapters is one that connects students to their communities while honoring and making space for fascination and personal initiative, which is every individual's birthright. Teachers who dip their toes into journalistic learning will discover that it's possible to manage the complexity and intensity of a "real-world" project while letting go of the need to control the outcome. They will see that students thrive when they are allowed to draw from the well of their own curiosity in order to follow a question and make sense of what they notice, experience, and wonder about.

I know, as do the authors of this timely book, that young people who are given meaningful opportunities to question the status quo and to navigate the currents of our often confusing, information-saturated era always move forward with not just practical skills, but with greater self-assurance and a more nuanced understanding of the world and themselves. What a rare, memorable, even life-changing, gift.

Esther Wojcicki
founder of Palo Alto Media Arts Program, cofounder of the Journalistic
Learning Initiative at University of Oregon, chief academic adviser
to Pressto.ai, and former chair creative at Commons.org

INTRODUCTION: WHY JOURNALISTIC LEARNING?

Another book and another so-called revolutionary approach? Is this the peda-gogical flavor of the month? You may be asking yourself, "Why should I care?"

Students sit in class asking themselves the same questions. "Why do I need to study this?" "How is this relevant to my life?" "Why should I care?"

To be sure, young students often struggle to see how the curriculum will help them in the future, but it's worth addressing this classic student refrain by briefly stepping into their shoes. What did you care about when you were in middle or high school?

Were you curious about fashion design or intrigued by the possibilities of space travel? Were you a big football fan and always eager for the recess bell to ring, or were you really into art and happy to stay inside on weekends? Maybe you wanted to be a veterinarian, a guitarist, or an architect. Perhaps you were concerned about politics, the environment, or changing social norms.

Take another moment to think about how often this particular interest—whatever it may have been—was honored in your middle or high school class-room. Did your English or social studies teachers honor those interests and allow you and your classmates to pursue such topics in any meaningful way? It's likely the answer is no.

For decades, our education system has treated many students, particularly in low-income schools, as passive receptors of information and demanded their teachers follow rigid curriculums that ignore innate curiosities and undermine a drive to learn. In essence, students were taught what to learn, not how to learn.

This factory-based framework may have made sense at the height of the industrial revolution when the country needed schools to prepare students for work on the assembly line, but it's increasingly irrelevant in our commu-nication-driven world. Today, people want and need to think creatively and express their concerns with confidence and authority.

Our Pilot Program

In 2015, Esther Wojcicki and Ed Madison cofounded the Journalistic Learning Initiative (JLI), a nonprofit education organization, with the financial support of Tara Guber and piloted a program to disrupt this factory model. We intentionally use the term journalistic rather than journalism, because, as we will detail, our approach expands beyond traditional school newspapers and magazines. We worked with sixth-graders in both language arts and social studies classes at a middle school in a small, rural town on the West Coast. Simultaneously, we launched a similar program in a neighboring high school.

Both schools are near Eugene, where coauthor Ed Madison teaches and is a researcher at the University of Oregon's School of Journalism and Communication (SOJC) with affiliated faculty status in the College of Education, coauthor and 20-year veteran English and journalism teacher Melissa Wantz resides, and coauthor and former classroom teacher Rachel Guldin earned her PhD. Former team member, Jordan Tichenor, supported these efforts. The methods were informed by the work of education thought leader Esther Wojcicki and her Palo Alto High School journalism program, which Ed studied for his dissertation.

The intent behind our research was to improve engagement, collaboration, and writing skills through a student-driven approach that validated and built upon their intrinsic interests. Students at both schools formed groups of three or four and investigated topics that intrigued them. Some researched ways to address homelessness, while others examined the ethics of animal cruelty in scientific research. On interview day, with press passes and reporters' notebooks, students engaged with experts and community members, both in person and via video chats. After 10 weeks of research, interviews, writing, and editing, they published their findings in web articles.

Compared with traditional schooling, journalistic learning may be the sole curricular experience where students are permitted and encouraged to connect with their community through project-based storytelling for an authentic audience (not just for their teacher). Our 2016 pilot aimed to see how this innovative approach improved writing and affected broader academic outcomes, particularly for students attending underserved schools, including schools with low-income and racially or ethnically diverse populations.

Insights gathered from both pilot programs informed the development of the *Effective Communicators* course, an educational supplement created by JLI that implements the journalistic learning tools and techniques explored in this book. Independent external evaluations and peer-reviewed research affirm that the program significantly improves students' ability to think critically, collaborate, and persist to complete writing assignments (Madison et al., 2019).

The participating sixth-grade English and social studies teacher saw first-hand how these discussions impacted students beyond the pilot program: "Having a class in rows and having students raise their hands isn't the only way to run a classroom. To observers, it may look chaotic. But if you look deeper, kids are learning."

One of her students, who is on the autism spectrum, seemed to perform better during journalistic learning sessions. He was typically shy and unengaged in most of his classes. The teacher and his classmates accommodated by giving him the freedom to roam and fidget without reprimand or embarrassment. Still, he often lagged behind his peers academically. This teacher found the student was more focused during our Thursday sessions, where he contributed to his team's research efforts and helped choose an expert to address their topic. Passionate about video games, the team identified and sought to interview the designer of one of their favorite games. They researched the company's website, found a name, and mustered the courage to call and connect. To their amazement, a receptionist put them through, and within minutes they were able to speak with an expert source and extend an invitation to interview day.

Rather than focus the interview on game play, the student asked the video game expert sophisticated questions about entering the game design field: How many years of schooling does it require, and how much salary can one make? The student exhibited a new sense of leadership and focus, and his teacher found he became more confident in sharing with his peers outside of these special Thursday meetings.

On another day, the teacher engaged her students in a discussion about cultural sensitivity in relation to India's caste system. She asked her sixth-graders to consider appropriate ways to hypothetically interview individuals living within the more impoverished realms of the system: "If you were going to interview a Dalit, for example, how would you phrase your question?"

Understandably, many students said they felt uncomfortable asking a poor person direct questions about their living situation or financial standing. They feared such questions would offend. Just after one student voiced this opinion, the teacher noticed the student with autism erasing one of the answers. It was obvious that he had a different perspective, but like many middle schoolers, he wanted to fit in and was choosing to adopt the consensus view.

The teacher viewed this as a potentially valuable moment. She wanted to validate the student's hastily erased response. With ease, she asked, "What was the answer you erased?"

The student said he believed, if asked with compassion, it was perfectly all right to ask about living in poverty. This was a perspective gained from his personal experience. "He comes from a low socioeconomic family, and he thought that would be OK," the teacher noted. She reassured him and the class that answers aren't always simply right or wrong. Nuance factors into some situations. Sometimes, the appropriateness of a question depends on tone and intent. "When I gave him the time to actually say what he thought, I mean, it may have changed other people's thinking and kind of changed my thinking a little bit too," the teacher recounted.

A Journalistic Approach to Secondary Language Arts

Such examples illustrate that exploring topics through a journalistic lens— one that foregrounds asking questions of oneself and one's source—can illuminate and broaden students' and instructors' perspectives. It's also an approach that upends a traditional classroom paradigm that can often be constrained by one-sided dissemination of information.

With journalistic learning, teachers aren't gatekeepers of knowledge or overseers of the content but trusted guides, letting students make their own discoveries while helping them connect their new understanding to existing knowledge. This approach also helps students become confident communicators, develops their resiliency, and allows them to realize the innate power of their own voices.

These skills are needed more than ever. Think of all the turmoil students endured as they navigated perilous months and years in our nation's history. As the COVID-19 pandemic raged, millions of teenagers were stuck at home in isolation, kept away from friends, clubs, sports, and, of course, the classroom. Marginalized students in rural areas and underserved communities of color had an especially difficult time, often not having adequate internet access to engage meaningfully with live instruction. Following George Floyd's murder, these same students experienced the most significant and widespread movement for racial justice in generations. And in the fall of 2020, they lived through one of the most contentious presidential elections in American history (Schulten, 2022).

These are difficult topics to unpack, to be sure, but it would be a disservice if we failed to provide students with the conceptual foundation and tools to discuss them in a meaningful way. Young people care about these and other serious topics and want to have these conversations, and they *are* having them—outside of class without thoughtful guidance. In a classroom where students lead inquiry and research, controversial current events allow teachers to model respectful discourse and self-reflection. Media literacy is more essential than ever.

Education leaders are responding. In April 2022, the National Council of Teachers of English (NCTE) published a position paper, "Media Education in English Language Arts," calling for English teachers to bring media education into language arts classrooms:

> For students to be prepared for success in college and careers, they need high levels of engagement in their own learning and a strong sense of confidence in their identity as learners. For this reason, media education pedagogies can be a key lever in education reform when educators wield influence in ways that support critical, flexible, responsive, and creative thinking.
>
> NCTE advocates for students to have time to engage regularly with three core themes:
>
> 1. Exploring representation and power with critical reading, listening, and viewing
> 2. Empowering voice with writing, speaking, and self-expression
> 3. Increasing relevance by critically examining digital media and popular culture

Journalistic learning is made to order to fulfill these needs.

We've titled this book *Language Arts in Action* because it aptly describes how language arts can be applied in service of helping our students make sense of our complex world. Distinct from literature, poetry, and other genres of writing, journalism is English put to work.

This book explains our project-based approach, one that has been adapted and used successfully by secondary teachers in dozens of secondary language arts classrooms. Since 2015, JLI has positively impacted the academic outcomes of more than 7,500 middle and high school students in Oregon, Washington, Idaho, Arizona, and California. The *Effective Communicators* course is an outgrowth of research, experimentation, and classroom experience.

The program itself is based on a four-part framework, emphasizing voice, agency, publication, and reflection:

1. *Voice* means showing students that their thoughts, opinions, investigations, concerns, and experiences matter in the classroom, while teaching them the practical, transferable skills that help them develop lifelong confidence in speaking, listening, and writing.

2. *Agency* means showing students how their writing and voice can make an impact and influence others. Much of the research underpinning journalistic learning originates from self-determination theory. This concept asserts we aren't solely motivated by rewards or deterred by punishment. We have innate desires and ambitions, as well as an innate drive for intellectual and psychological growth.

3. *Publication* means creating pathways for students to share their work outside the classroom, thus connecting them with their wider community. They aren't simply turning in their assignments for grades; they are creating work that matters, possibly even work that spurs change.

4. *Reflection* means having students examine their beliefs, their community, and their growth over time and how they will move through the world in all its complexity and challenges, both now and in the future.

We will address these components in more detail in Chapter 2.

You don't need to have previously taught journalism to adopt this approach in your language arts classroom, nor do we presuppose your students will pursue a career in journalism after school. Likewise, journalistic learning in a language arts setting will not compete for resources, as these strategies are meant to be adopted and adapted into existing English language arts classrooms. Also, this work will not compete with your school's existing student media program. In fact, some of your students may discover they are interested in journalism as an elective, feeding new energy into existing publications.

Most of us consume journalism in our daily lives, whether it's in a mobile newsfeed, on a broadcast, or through a podcast. The strategies detailed here build on that familiarity and allow you to personalize instruction to fit your teaching style and your students' needs. With permission to explore topics that align with their authentic interests, students become visibly more invested in their own learning.

LANGUAGE ARTS
IN ACTION

CHAPTER 1

Communication Is Critical to Students' Futures

"Teaching today's students the same material in the same manner as I was taught 35 years ago would be not only detrimental but almost unethical."

—High School English Teacher

THE WORLD SEEMS AT ODDS. Our leaders no longer reliably model civil discourse, and we appear increasingly unable to reach consensus about vital common concerns. It seems as if our social fabric is at risk of fraying with each passing day. If our cherished system of government is to survive, students need opportunities to practice democracy—the thoughtful weighing of opposing viewpoints—while in community. Journalistic projects fulfill that aim.

Children are born journalists. They possess the two essential components of any dogged reporter: an inquisitive mind and a need to share what they learn with a larger audience.

Much like professional journalists, they seek out the experts. Think of young children peppering their parents, grandparents, older siblings, neighbors, and teachers with questions about how the natural world works around them: How do fish breathe underwater? How hot is the sun? What do clouds feel like?

As we grow up, modern life—and the modern school system—has a way of inadvertently discouraging individual lines of inquiry and dampening these curiosities. Bright and curious students move in lockstep through middle and high school in an education system that for the sake of efficiency often demands that they abandon their own interests and conform to rigid academic constructs. Educators also face curricular and structural constraints, unable to give their students enough time to deeply explore their interests.

Educator and philosopher Paulo Freire (2018) calls this the "banking model," in which students are understood as empty vessels waiting to be filled with knowledge. This model has dominated educational thinking for over a century. Decades of standardized testing and test preparation have led students to surmise there's usually one right answer to a question and perhaps only one way to view an issue.

Brilliant and caring teachers have resisted and challenged this model, of course, viewing the classroom as a place for investigation and exploration. Freire calls this more open-ended approach the "problem-posing model," in which students are understood as agentic and knowledgeable, and teachers and students learn together through critical thinking, questioning, and discussion. Striving to widen their students' minds, teachers engage with bold inquiry. They reach well beyond the four walls of the classroom, despite the curricular constraints.

One such teacher was Ray "Bud" McFetridge at Riverside Elementary School in Roseburg, Oregon. In 1960 he led his fourth-grade students to try to venture well beyond our country's borders by attempting to find them pen pals in what was then the Soviet Union.

This assignment perfectly blended curiosity and communication. On the one hand, the project provided an opportunity to understand a contemporary issue: the Cold War. At the same time, the project aimed to foster understanding between two seemingly disparate groups of children during an era shrouded in distrust. Or it would have if the U.S. State Department hadn't denied the fourth-grade class secretary Janice Boyle's request for Russian schoolchildren contacts.

Nearly 60 years later, in 2019, a small reporting class at the University of Oregon School of Journalism and Communication devoted itself to the challenge of tracking down the young fourth-grader who had asked permission to write letters to her Russian peers.

Their professor, Peter Laufer (an award-winning journalist and colleague of Ed's), happened upon a brief article in the online archives of the New York Times detailing the State Department's 1960 denial. Believing it would give his students the opportunity to practice locating sources, he told them to find that girl.

Not only did the student journalists find and interview Janice Boyle (now 70 years old and living in Las Vegas), they also obtained F.B.I. files on the incident through a Freedom of Information Act request, which gave them insight into the political rationale behind the State Department's actions. Eventually, the college journalists carried letters from current Oregon fourth-graders to a class of Russian schoolchildren, establishing a friendly connection between international citizens—a connection the American government had denied the Roseburg class almost 60 years before and one made more poignant with the escalation of the Russian war against Ukraine in 2022.

We recount this story here and ask teachers to share it with their students to illustrate how a group of undergraduates, not much older than middle and high school students themselves, can produce thoughtful and engaging work, especially when they have an encouraging guide. These novices were capable of conducting the often-tricky task of original inquiry and shoe-leather reporting and were themselves surprised by what they achieved. *The New York Times* wrote a feature on their investigation, and the students published a book titled *Classroom 15: How the Hoover FBI Censored the Dreams of Innocent Oregon Fourth Graders* (2020).

Connecting Schoolwork with Authentic Interests

Of course, we're not expecting your middle or high school students to file Freedom of Information requests. Nor, for that matter, are we suggesting you send them on flights to Russia. What we are suggesting is that you help them connect their genuine interests to the larger, messier, surprising world that exists beyond any textbook or curriculum. Journalistic learning opens unexpected doors.

Many teachers already discuss emerging international or national news stories in class. But you can take it a step further. You can, for example, ask students to bring in meaningful local news stories to share with peers. Even better, you can ask them to come to class with examples of local problems and challenge them to go beyond the complaining stage to serious questioning, followed by investigation and reporting.

Students are citizens within their communities—which bears repeating, as indisputable as it may sound. They are impacted by the issues facing their community, and yet their concerns are seldom heard outside of school. They often have questions that go unasked: *Why are rents going up so fast, and what can be done about it? How do phones affect student mental health? Is college really for everyone?*

Now you're giving them autonomy over some of their content.

Communication is central to the program we've constructed. Human interaction lies at the heart of nearly all the activities and exercises we've developed.

Working in groups, students collaborate to produce and publish meaningful news articles and accompanying websites. But the journey begins with individual reflection: *What am I worried about? What do I notice that needs more attention?* Next comes discussion and consensus: *This is what we wonder. This is what we will investigate.* Finding an issue that matters and grabs your attention is relatively simple, but finding a single issue everyone in your team can agree to pursue for the remainder of a project can be tricky. Your students will need to reconcile differences and set a common goal.

Additionally, students seek out a local expert on their chosen issue, a source they can invite to class and interview in front of peers. They learn the art of interviewing: *How can we get the most informative answers from our expert? How can we convince them to answer our questions in the first place?*

Students also produce rough drafts of their stories and share them with peers outside of their reporting group: *How can we offer feedback without discouraging our friends? How can we accept feedback to make our work better or reject feedback that we don't agree with?*

At every stage of the work cycle, students practice communication. They talk with each other; they talk with people in the community. They write for each other; they write to and for people in the community.

Good communication is, after all, essential for journalists to successfully do their jobs. They need to talk with their editors about deadlines and artfully articulate their story pitches. They need to nail down meetings with sources and strategically plan their questions ahead of time. They need to convey not only the key elements of their story but their process—how they acquired their information—to establish trust with their readers.

Journalism isn't the only career that demands good communication skills. Many professions require good listening and speaking. Think of interior designers who interview clients hoping to update a kitchen, carefully listening to their ideas while also unveiling their own practical vision. Think of veterinarians who, at times, must balance consolation and support with clear options for addressing the pain of a beloved pet.

The communications approach and project outlined in this book ask students to work with multiple groups, collaborating to refine pitches, rough drafts, and website designs. Throughout this process, you'll be their guide, not the primary purveyor of knowledge. Students will make discoveries together about their chosen issue and collaborate to share knowledge with their community, ultimately contributing to the online media landscape that they navigate daily only as consumers.

Developing Media Literacy

For student researchers, this online world is an unkempt mess, riddled with slippery, even harmful, rabbit holes. Go deep enough in one, and it can be hard to dig out. Gone are the days of media gatekeepers who tried to allow only verified information out into the world. Today, teachers need to help prepare students for the misinformation and disinformation that pollute the social media landscape. Students must learn, as we describe in Chapter 2, not only how to discern news from opinion online, but how to discern between stories grounded in reality and stories disengaged from it.

The National Council of Teachers of English (NCTE) acknowledges the need for change in its 2022 position paper, "Media Education in English Language Arts":

> Research evidence amply shows the need to move beyond the exclusive focus on traditional reading and writing competencies. For example, secondary school students lack critical reading comprehension skills that require them to distinguish between journalism and sponsored content, and they routinely ignore the source of a message when judging its accuracy. (Breakstone et al., 2019)

Inquiry around complex current issues requires thoughtful questioning, listening, and sharing, especially while navigating a social media landscape that incentivizes the building and maintenance of information echo chambers. Search engine algorithms filter results based on our "likes" and "retweets," and increasingly social media measures the number of seconds we spend looking at a post, sending similar posts into our feeds. This reinforces and hardens our views rather than challenging and expanding them.

For proof, just look at the coverage of the biggest news story of the past few years: the COVID-19 pandemic. Consider all the conspiracy theories that took root amid COVID-19's rise. Bad actors operating online sowed doubt over the virus' origins and trumpeted fraudulent treatments for it.

Students should be asked in school to critically analyze broad media coverage. *How did different media outlets cover an issue? What facts, for example, did an outlet include in a story? Who did reporters talk to? Who didn't they talk to? What are other outlets saying about the same topic?* Students who have practiced scanning information for bias and who can distinguish fact from rumor (or even better, who can ask themselves what was left out of the story) will gain agency and power over disinformation and be more critical consumers of news for the rest of their lives (Hobbs, 2020).

Additionally, students should learn that the media aren't a single entity, even though we often speak as if they are. They're an industry of competing newspapers, magazines, digital publications, podcasts, and broadcast and cable news channels. To dismiss a news story by saying "the media is lying to you," is just as lazy as blithely accepting dubious claims from your social media feed.

During a 2013 commencement speech at Wake Forest University, trailblazing journalist Gwen Ifill once described the difference between cynicism and skepticism this way: "Cynics think they know the answers already, and then they stop listening. Skeptics always have more questions to ask, but we are willing to be persuaded to the honesty of an alternative point of view."

At heart, journalists are skeptics. Teenagers usually are, too. It's a natural fit.

We believe a journalistic learning project can help your students begin the challenging yet rewarding journey of questioning what they read and watch online while creating ribbons of awareness about community problems and solutions. Teaching students to question and actively listen will serve them well as they research their chosen issues, and it will also help them become more empathetic in their daily communication. The journalistic approach to learning helps students recognize the humanity in someone holding an opposing view.

Think of the insights those Roseburg fourth-graders could have gathered had they been permitted to write to their Russian peers. No, their letters likely wouldn't have resolved the differences each student felt about their peer's country, but they could have shared with their pen pals their own experiences at school and learned their beliefs, worries, and hopes. As Ifill might agree, they could have been persuaded by the honesty of their peer's perspectives and filled a void with just a little understanding. This is why communication matters.

CHAPTER 2

Leveraging the Journalistic Learning Framework

"I knew that I needed to do something different, something that was authentic that I could get the students to write in a way they cared about."

—English Teacher

TEACHERS OF ADOLESCENTS KNOW students are inconsistent. They swing emotionally from two poles: the safety of their experienced childhood truths, which can feel like the most certain and all-encompassing permanent knowledge, and their growing suspicion that imminent adulthood is not orderly like the seasons, but rather is indeterminate and unpredictable, like the number of branches a sapling will one day grow.

At one moment in the English classroom—maybe after explicating the poem "The Road Not Taken" or discussing Winston's self-destructive motives in the novel *1984*—students can show a level of vulnerability and openness to new ideas that takes your breath away. In the next, you witness impenetrable mental rigidity and unwillingness to question their own misgivings or clichéd beliefs about people, society, and the world.

If six weeks spent unpacking themes in books like *To Kill a Mockingbird* or *The House on Mango Street* doesn't challenge students to develop a more nuanced understanding of how human problems are born, persist, and grow systemic, what can?

For one student in a sixth-grade English language arts and social studies class at a rural middle school, the path to a more complex view of humanity and community problems was found by taking on the role of journalist.

At the start of the class project, one boy and three other 11-year-olds found themselves in a reporting team tasked with choosing an issue of concern, then researching local aspects of the issue, interviewing local sources, and writing an objective news article based on their findings. They chose the topic of homelessness.

The boy's mindset at the beginning of the project was simple and biased. He believed most homeless people were lazy abusers of public services. When asked to reflect on the experience two years later as an eighth-grader, he said:

> All of my opinions were very strong back then. My whole thing was, "if you're homeless it's your fault. Sorry, buddy. Deal with it." But I actually realized some people can't help what situations they're in and that some form of government assistance can get them going, and they can become self-sufficient.

It was through interviewing a shelter care manager that the student learned young people his age can experience homelessness through no fault of their own when their families suffer sudden economic or health-related crises. His team's research and reporting were later published online, as were all of the articles produced by students in the class.

For this student, this was not just a school assignment that built language arts skills; it was a character-building project with potentially lasting impact. For the rest of his life, there is a good chance that when he sees an unhoused person, he will think, feel, and respond to that person with deeper understanding, knowing from his own classroom experience that he is a person who can change his mind about original beliefs.

Teachers who adopt the journalistic approach not only help their students cohesively build critical reading, researched writing, effective speaking, and close listening skills, they also prepare their students to become more engaged citizens, ready to navigate our complex, evolving, and ever-expanding information landscape.

Students are given methods to research and fact-check claims, and they learn to effectively explore and inquire. This builds competence. As they direct their own learning, under careful and supportive supervision, they begin to feel capable of tackling other novel challenges.

Students develop a new sense of awareness about societal issues and the realization they can play a role in shining light on these concerns. They also can change their attitudes toward the news.

The path to this kind of discovery starts with helping students identify and assert their convictions through voice, agency, publication, and reflection.

Before we examine and explain the four principles that frame the approach, we should pause to review how journalistic learning differs from other writing projects commonly taught in the English classroom.

What Journalistic Learning Isn't

In journalistic writing, students are not crafting narrative, persuasive, or response-to-literature essays. They aren't assigned or arbitrarily picked to represent one side of an issue. They aren't forced to adhere to a five-paragraph organizational structure. They are not provided source material in advance. The teacher doesn't assign current events, literature, or any specific texts to serve as the basis of student research.

The journalistic process produces writing that is informative, fact-based, well-sourced, and not autobiographical (although students may draw on their personal experiences to discover the issues that matter to them).

This approach favors local research on local issues that matter right now. The topics students select relate to current concerns facing their own community. While the issues may coexist at national and global levels, like climate change, the focus of research is local. This shift might change a central question from *What can we do about climate change?* to *How is our city preparing for future storm flooding connected to climate change?*

The articles students produce are not written for the teacher but for the public and must meet key journalistic standards and news conventions that value fact over opinion and demand thoughtful but fair weighing of different points of view. This means conducting interviews with local experts.

For example, one boy and one girl in a rural middle school chose to report on the issue of racism. *What's being done about it? How have things changed?* In front of the class they interviewed the president of the local NAACP chapter, who responded with insight on their community, offering personal experience not found in a textbook.

Interviewing local experts strengthens students' connection to (and hopefully faith in) their community. These interactions foster shared understanding, build trust, and help students see that they are stakeholders too.

Finally, journalistic student writing does not languish in a teacher's turn-in basket or ultimately in the depths of a backpack or computer folder. It is published on public-facing websites that students create. It's shareable to peers, parents, and extended family, as well as to the experts they interviewed. A shift happens in the class culture as students realize they aren't merely building skills to use in college or later in life; they are contributing to the public good right now.

The Four Principles of the Framework

What, then, is journalistic learning? For a better understanding of the process, let's unpack the four principles of journalistic learning: voice, agency, publication, and reflection, which you can see in Figure 2.1.

Voice

The first principle in journalistic learning is honoring student voice: showing young people that their ideas, concerns, and experiences matter. The process starts by challenging students to understand that they may not know enough at any given time to form an accurate opinion.

Typically, this happens in the initial discussions of the newly formed reporting teams. There, they state what they know about their chosen topic, as well as examine their own biases. It can be a fraught time. Students may want to speak more than listen, or they might try to recede into passive silence. They may want to control the outcome—what they believe the article should say—

FIGURE 2.1 **The pedagogy of journalistic learning revolves around four principles that support student voice and stories.**

Credit: The Journalistic Learning Initiative

rather than examine the vastness of the research problem. They may start to suspect that their understanding is far less than they thought and that their chosen issue is unnervingly complex.

Personalities can clash at this stage.

"I can be known as kind of a control freak," a sixth-grader admitted, reflecting on his work with peers. "I tend to have an idea that I think is a really good idea, and sometimes the rest of my group doesn't think it's a good idea."

Showing admirable self-awareness for a sixth-grader, this student admitted to being headstrong, but when it came time a bit later in the project to interview a community source in front of the class, rather than stifle his strident voice, his teacher coached him to consider how he might help his group develop a respectful line of questions.

Because American students are no strangers to argumentative writing and discussion, which is practiced in the very early grades, the student and his peers were adept in offering energetic opinions.

The journalistic learning project helped them understand that passionate opinion does not outweigh cold, hard facts. The students were challenged at various stages by new information, new voices, and budding awareness of just how much they assumed but didn't know was true.

Ultimately, they were able to set aside personal feelings and build consensus around what the facts were and what information deserved to be published.

A journalistic learning approach also helps students understand abstract issues in a more tangible way. Homelessness, food insecurity, and racial discrimination hit differently when students learn people they know and like are affected. This happened with a coreporter on the same homelessness project. She said:

"It really just opened my eyes to people in my community who could need help and are showing the signs, but most of us don't see it."

Coming to grips with these realities builds empathy and provides students with opportunities to step outside of their personal concerns and develop compassion for and interest in others.

Students also cultivate a collective voice, as a reporting team. A middle school teacher stated:

"I think that they like what they're doing. I feel like they think that they have a voice and that they're actually doing something."

One principal described how students at his high school discovered their voices through journalistic learning, which began in a single class in 2016 and expanded throughout the school's English curriculum:

"I think that the ability to express yourself in a way that you never thought you could or thought possible . . . it's a great skill to have."

Agency

One sixth-grader who reported on racism is biracial and was one of the few Black students in the 2016 pilot program. As part of their research, he and his reporting team encountered websites with examples of hateful speech. He noted:

"Obviously you know about racism, but you think about segregation back in the 60s and Martin Luther King . . . I didn't realize that today, there's racism in newer forms."

A white classmate reacted with compassion:

"I care for my friend, and don't see why anyone would want to promote such hate."

It's not easy for teachers to help students navigate tough and controversial topics or to support parents in helping their children make sense of these issues in a safe and empathetic setting, but there is no alternative in a democracy. Ideas must be presented for public discourse, and certainly by middle and high school all students need to learn how to talk respectfully about hard things, setting emotions aside when necessary, in order to deeply listen and understand alternative views. Journalistic learning provides teachers with an adaptable method.

Whereas most school assignments are initiated by teachers, journalistic assignments originate with students. Buy-in increases significantly as students develop a deeper sense of ownership around assignments they cocreate with peers.

Journalistic learning also connects adolescents with the adults in their community who drive change. Agency can be personal, as well. Inspired by his research on racism, the biracial student in our pilot program chose to grow out his hair in the form of an Afro that year. Two years later, he reflected on his reasons:

"When there was segregation, people of color grew out their hair to show power. It definitely has me embrace my ethnicity, because it shows that I'm proud to be an African American student."

Students engaged in journalistic writing also challenge perceived limitations and biases about the capabilities of adolescent learners. They choose topics that are more difficult than adults might assign. They formulate questions that adults might not expect. And they connect with community members and professionals as equals. The principal at a small rural middle school shared:

> It's awesome seeing our sixth-graders as they're interviewing on Skype there. Their engagement level is very high [. . .] they're just not used to doing something like this where they're actively interviewing people [. . .] and they're taking notes. I go out to the playground with them at lunch time. They're kids, they're acting like, you know, 11- and 12-year-olds. And then in the classroom I see these really professional respectful interviews and [they're] just taking it to another level.

Journalistic learning stretches students to think about the future and their own role in advocating for solutions to big problems. One sixth-grader said that the project caused her to see herself anew. She felt more confident and interested in the world. And she came to believe she and her friends in class had more power than they had imagined to investigate and think about what could be done to make their future better.

Publication

Sharing writing with an authentic local audience separates the journalistic approach from other forms of scholastic work. When they realize peers, family, and community members will view their articles, will fact-check their information, and will learn from sources they interview, students tend to bring an increased commitment and energy to writing.

Publishing is the special sauce in an English language arts classroom: it allows students to see their agency and voice in the real world. Their work becomes less transactional and more meaningful when done as a public service versus for points toward a grade. A sense of pride and teamwork develops that may seem more like being in the band, on a soccer team, or in a speech and debate club. As writers, they're in the game, on the field, and at the podium, not just endlessly practicing.

The principal at one urban high school said he sees students who learn through the journalistic learning approach realize their own potential through publication. He said:

> They were able to work on something collaboratively and put it out there for others to see, and say, "that's mine" and "I put my name on that" or

"I was part of that" or "I was the brainstorm or the brainchild behind it." There's a ton of ownership, and what I think that does for kids is it helps them actualize what they're capable of.

Students also discover that publishing their work, especially if their sources will be reading it, requires an extra layer of responsibility to get it right.

The sixth-grader who coreported on homelessness, reflected years later that the journalistic approach caused her to step it up in school:

I always kind of goofed around and would write at home, but I never really took it seriously until then. And then, it got me really excited for the future. It really made me think that there could be a future in writing for me.

Sometimes the publication experience catches fire among students and they take it even further. This was the experience for a 10th-grade English teacher at a rural high school. His students felt inspired and empowered to write grants to fund the creation of a glossy paper magazine designed to capture the ethos of their generation. He recalled:

There's this magical thing that happened where they kind of took this exponential leap. It was all based on what they wanted to do. It's not like I had a list of, like, "here are stories you can do." They naturally pitched them and reported, researched, and crafted this magazine. It's just a really cool moment for these kids to kind of step into a space where it felt like a real publication.

Having students experience the power of publication doesn't require a budget or award-winning design skills.

This teacher and his students made do with a nearly decade-old desktop computer donated from the local university's journalism school. Their publication won his students top honors in a national competition, and they raised additional funds to travel out of state to accept their award.

At one rural middle school, sixth-grade students also worked on desktop computers with outdated operating systems. An open-space library area doubled as a computer lab, shared by the entire school on a rotating basis. Students published their work to the internet using a platform-agnostic free tool with attractive graphic templates that made novice design work look professional.

Free website publishing platforms give teachers and students flexibility, professional-looking templates, and wide reach. During journalistic learning, students also are coached to decide how and when to responsibly share their completed work on social media, further amplifying their voices and reaching broader audiences.

Reflection

As the final component of the framework, reflection is where students consider what they've learned, how their understanding has grown and changed, what deeper meaning they've encountered, and how they've grown in the process. Reflection requires thoughtfulness and introspection, a stepping back from the daily process to consider any broader or deeper impacts.

Students are asked to reflect at many points of the project. When first coalescing around an issue with their reporting team, for example, they are asked to examine their own biases about the topic and determine if they can adopt a neutral stance to research and write about it.

Another point of reflection centers on news ethics. Students are asked early on to reflect on "sponsored content," the sophisticated paid advertising that many people mistake for journalism. It's everywhere now, from their local paper to *The New York Times*, and it gets harder to recognize every year. Journalistic learning asks them to question why news outlets don't ban confusing sponsored content and stick with traditional ads that everyone knows are advertising. What is the media's responsibility to the public versus their own bottom lines?

Some of the most meaningful reflection for students centers on their own performance in class. After their interviews, they are asked to determine what went well and what could have gone better. What norms did they follow or forget? How could better preparation have helped? Did they show active listening and ask the types of questions that cause sources to open up?

Prior to turning in a final draft of their writing, students reflect on the journalistic best practices they have learned, from balancing sources to attributing information to including quantitative details. This is followed by an end-of-course written reflection in which they compare their understanding of the news on the first day of the project with their understanding now.

Along the way, students are encouraged to be honest about what they notice in the news. Some feel their voices are not represented by news organizations or that their communities are unjustly covered. After a lesson on newsroom ethics, they may well question what they see across the media spectrum. *Is it fair? Whom does this serve? Does it harm or help? Whose voices are included and whose are left out?*

Through written reflection, students tend to want to interpret the potential impact of their work, which is usually not the case with a typical English essay that goes no further than the teacher's desk.

Why Journalistic Learning Now?

Resilience may be the most critical quality we can nurture in students at this time. The world they're inheriting offers far fewer certainties than when we were teenagers. The unprecedented levels of anxiety and depression reported by students aren't unfounded. They reflect valid concerns about global pandemics, economic instability, gun violence, and the very survival of the planet, to name a few.

While novels and short stories often explore tough universal themes, students in language arts classes also seek more immediate ways to make sense of daily life. They want to unpack what's happening now, as serious challenges unfold in real time on their social media feeds and television screens. Teaching language arts through a journalistic lens can meet that need.

Instructors, too, understand that they could use new ways to guide adolescents to read critically, research responsibly, and write effectively. Many teachers would like better ideas for assessing essential speaking and listening standards than assigning students yet another PowerPoint presentation. They long to watch their students do meaningful work, like interviewing the mayor in front of the class.

In *Raising Student Voice* by Katherine Schulten (2020), a high school teacher named Sarah Gross in New Jersey shares her concern about the times we teach in:

> I sometimes feel like a majority of my ninth-graders are getting their "news" from conspiracy-theory stuff on YouTube. At home and in school, we adults focus on things like "Don't share your private info online"—but they're way, way beyond that. The answer is not saying, "Wikipedia and Reddit are not credible sources." We need to teach them to read everything critically. My 13-and 14-year-olds have been on Fortnite and browsing Reddit since they were 10, but they haven't read a newspaper, for the most part, until they sit down in my class. (p. 40)

Journalistic learning broadens the average teenager's information diet by helping them find and vet credible sources. It guides them to read critically and share valid information on the issues they care about. It shows them how ethical news is made, which prepares them to use discernment in their own reading, viewing, and sharing.

Understanding a Project-Based Approach

As new technologies help classrooms connect quickly and easily to the world outside of school, many teachers are eager to implement student-centered projects. In her book *Real Learning, Real Work* (1997), Boston-area teacher and educational program designer Adria Steinberg identified six design principles for project-based learning and offered educators a compelling alternative to the lecture, practice, assess approach that felt increasingly fragmented, simplistic, and instructor-centered. Steinberg called these the Six A's, which we summarize here:

1. *Authentic:* The project centers on a problem meaningful to students. They attempt to answer a question that an adult in the community might also ask and produce writing that has personal and social value beyond the school setting.
2. *Academically rigorous:* The project develops higher order thinking. Students use the same methods and thought processes that professionals use.
3. *Applied learning:* The project requires students to practice the organizational skills expected in collaborative, high-performing work organizations, using modern technology tools.
4. *Active exploration:* The project asks students to use a variety of methods, media, and sources in a real investigation with an unknown outcome.
5. *Adult relationships:* The project connects students with adult community experts.
6. *Assessment:* The project results in students publishing their understanding for adults outside of school.

Built on the traditions of Dewey and Vygotsky, project-based learning asks students to "learn by doing" (Kersten, 2017, p. 34). Research shows that this type of learning is meaningful and effective for students in and out of the classroom (Bell, 2010). Nell K. Duke (2016), a professor of education at the University of Michigan, writes that project-based learning improves students' creative and critical thinking while improving their skills and knowledge. The authenticity of project-based learning is a meaningful factor for students. A 2019 study from Block and Strachan shows that elementary school students' writing improved when they wrote for a public audience instead of a teacher audience. In addition, research shows that students value the challenge of interdisciplinary project-based learning and find it meaningful (Virtue & Hinnant-Crawford, 2019).

The project-based approach of journalistic learning meets all of the Six A's (as does the practice of journalism itself). It targets 95% of the national English Language Arts College and Career Readiness standards (National Governors Association Center for Best Practices, Council of Chief State School Officers, 2010) (see Table A.1 in Appendix A). And it can be adapted for students between 6th and 12th grades, giving teachers who need to change grade levels or even move to a new school the flexibility to take the project with them. Research on journalistic learning shows that students have experienced intrinsic motivation, autonomy, and agentic and transformational growth (Guldin et al., 2021; Madison et al., 2019).

Acknowledging Barriers to Creating Learner-Centered Projects

Designing a high-caliber project-based unit can lead to rewarding professional experiences for teachers, especially if they collaborate with colleagues to create grade-wide projects that repeat and evolve from year to year. Students in schools where this happens feel the joy of intrinsically motivated learning and may even look forward to these projects well before they reach a teacher's class, a sign of how meaningful they were for previous learners.

However, teachers eager to design such projects face a universal problem: a lack of time. It can be exceptionally time-consuming and energy intensive to create from scratch a rigorous, comprehensive, student-centered project that meets state standards and district requirements while also teaching a full academic middle school or high school class load.

Building a new project may takes hours of focused planning time to:

- Identify the project scope and sequence
- Determine major and minor learning goals
- Align activities with learning standards

- Create individual lessons
- Develop and gather instructional materials
- Research and prepare technology tools
- Create assessments

Secondary teachers *might* have 7 to 10 hours of weekly prep, contracted work time not spent directly with students. However, these hours are also spent preparing for future lessons and cleaning up from the day, providing student feedback, studying emerging teaching practices and content in their subject area, and supporting students, families, and colleagues via email, telephone calls, and meetings.

Some teachers have 150 or more students, each with individual needs, and helping just a few of them a day outside of class time is enough to make daily prep time disappear. Unless school leadership has purposefully structured intensive planning time by arranging for substitute teachers or by modifying a traditional school schedule, it's nearly impossible to carve out 30 to 40 hours of focused design time during the school year to create new project-based learning experiences for students.

Additionally, some educators lack the confidence to design a comprehensive student-centered project. They may never have experienced rigorous project-based learning as students themselves, nor teamed with other teachers who have developed them. And they may not have learned how to create and field test student-centered curricular units during their pre-service education and training.

Finally, some teachers have been disappointed by their projects. Even the most thoughtfully designed units can have hidden structural flaws that emerge during instruction, when it's too late to make serious adjustments. This includes issues with pacing, where students feel their learning is too slow (boring) or too rushed (stressful). Weak organization can leave students feeling unmoored, confused, and isolated.

The opposite problem, over scaffolding, can cause students to feel the learning experience is just another set of teacher demands to complete in order to get a grade. Projects also can suffer from issues of agency and autonomy, where most decisions still implicitly rest with the teacher instead of the students. Perhaps hardest of all is when sensitively designed projects feel phony, with students sensing they are merely playacting rather than actively participating in the world's concerns.

While many large educational publishers try to provide teachers with project options in their curriculum packages, in our experience these are not the kinds of student-centered, flexible, high-interest problem-solving units we describe in this book. They are often designed to narrowly focus on a text or to develop a set of skills with outcomes measured by a standardized assessment rather than by an authentic audience of peers and adults outside of school. Even more rarely do publisher-packaged projects require students to seek out and connect with their community to learn directly from a source.

If the world of learning really has turned inside out, if it really is less passive, more immediate, and less teacher-centered than at any time in history, we need to diversify the teaching and learning pathways in the English language arts classroom exactly as called for by the NCTE.

The journalistic learning approach that we discuss over the next six chapters delivers. Each chapter builds on the one before to help you overcome every one of the above barriers and lead your class in a new way.

One student who coreported on the issue of homelessness in middle school reflected four years later on the project's impact: "That class really changed my outlook [on] life and seeing what these people can do just by writing. And how people can change other people's lives just by writing." "I want to help people, and if I can do that by writing, that would be magnificent."

CHAPTER 3

Launching Their Project

"I am looking for that one thing that guides their learning rather than me guiding their learning. I want to see the spark in their eyes when they find the topic that interests them."

—High School English Teacher

A WORLD CONNECTED—the "global village" prophesied in 1964 by media philosopher Marshall McLuhan—is, in many ways, ever present. Yet, despite our personal gadgetry and global internet access to others, a great many of us still feel disconnected. We can beam a photo around the world in seconds but may not really know many of our neighbors. Without a tangible sense of community, youth in particular are inclined to feel isolated, discouraged, and anxiety-ridden.

Mix in warranted fears about the world around us: geopolitical instability, global pandemics, climate crises, mental health concerns, gun violence—pick your predicament—it's all pretty bleak. Whereas students do benefit from learning to make sense of our ever-complex world, it can seem overwhelming at times.

One answer to the overwhelm is to narrow the locus of concern. In other words, when considering all of the global problems that we worry about every day, where and how do they intersect our own communities? *Who is affected? Who is helping? What solutions are in the works here?*

Helping students develop a local lens fosters civic engagement and exposes them to community concerns that may be otherwise unfamiliar, especially in cities and towns that are becoming news deserts, where cutbacks, closings, and consolidations have adversely affected local media coverage. Local interview subjects are likely to be accessible and eager to invest time in talking to students and supporting their community schools.

This chapter will help you launch a journalistic learning project on which your students will work during a school quarter or trimester in small reporting teams on a local issue of their choice. You'll learn how to organize student groups and provide learners with foundational understanding, including the purposes of communication, the differences between mass and local media, and the ethical principles that credible journalists follow. We'll give you some practical advice about how to guide students to explore an issue they care about, how to navigate uncomfortable topics, and how they can create a story pitch.

Balancing the Need for Control with Messy Original Inquiry

At the heart of the journalistic learning project is choice. Why? Because students invest time and dedication in assignments they generate. Students research, interview, and write over many weeks. The process is inquiry based, using modern technology tools and news literacy skills. It requires complex reading, listening, speaking, and writing. The outcome is generative: the creation of a never-before-seen news article that synthesizes local facts with community voices and opinions, published for an audience of peers and adults outside of school.

Students meet five deadlines:

1. Committing to a topic
2. Getting a source for a live interview
3. Conducting a live interview
4. Drafting and editing an article
5. Publishing the article

While these deadlines offer clear signposts for student progress, the instructional path of the project has a nonlinear feel. The work of a journalist is often one step forward, two steps back. A potential source agrees to be interviewed but later proves difficult to confirm. A claim that appears online in one place is contradicted somewhere else. This is the messy work of original inquiry.

Working on this type of project involves a level of problem solving that differs from what students may encounter in other classes. Students aren't choosing details from predetermined texts. The research challenges aren't hypothetical; they involve real people who may have other priorities and unexpected personalities. Students become detectives, discovering what has happened before and what might happen next, what is known and what is not yet known. They follow leads and make their own learning paths. A high school English teacher said:

What I like about this and what is different is that my juniors finally get to choose a project. They're involved from the very, very first step as active participants of the whole unit. I love that. They just lit up and they said "Really? We get to select our topic?" Because as 10th-graders, they were given one essay topic for their research, and the whole class had to dive into it. And many of them weren't interested. Now they feel really engaged, from the first moment.

Teachers may instinctively seek to exert control over the process; however, students benefit from having the freedom to fumble and engage with complexity.

Ron Beghetto, a prominent education and social psychology professor at Arizona State University who researches and writes on creativity in the classroom, speaks about what some of his colleagues refer to as "the tyranny of the lesson plan." He notes that "teachers often plan creativity out of their classrooms by following plans that are excessively structured" (Madison, 2015, p. 48).

Beghetto references a prevalent pattern of classroom interaction known as the "IRE pattern" (Mehan, 1979), an acronym for Initiate, Respond, and Evaluate. Students in this type of classroom quickly learn that their role is to wait for the teacher to pose a question, to raise a hand in response, to provide the expected answer, and then wait for validation.

Beghetto argues that this staid approach to teaching is inadequate in an age that is defined by an increasing sense of ambiguity and complexity in the world. It also leaves little room for spontaneity and bursts of rich, free-flowing interactions, the kind that ignite transformative learning experiences.

Breaking from an authoritative mindset allows teachers themselves to model courageous learning. Students benefit when instruction focuses on discovery rather than repeating expected, so-called right answers.

One sixth-grade English language arts teacher talked about her first experience with incorporating journalistic learning into her practice: "I'm okay with learning with the kids. That's what I'm learning about myself, that it's okay to discover with the kids. It actually makes it more interesting for me."

Zoom In, Zoom Out: Accepting the Feel of a Journalistic Learning Project

The zoom-in, zoom-out pedagogical design of a journalistic learning project is deliberate. Students start with identifying personal concerns that will drive their learning: *What do you care about right now? What annoys or worries you about your community, and what do you already know or think you know about it?*

Then they zoom out to consider the modern media as a whole, learning how to spot bias and misinformation and how to look for credible claims and sources. Before long, they zoom back in on their chosen issue in order to craft great questions to ask people in their own community.

It may be tempting to reorganize the experience for students so that it feels more linear and straightforward. For example, you may feel inclined to begin by covering all of the big picture concepts and practical skills before students choose a topic. However, we advise against this. Self-directed learning— whether it's completing a laser flip on a skateboard, creating a podcast, or mastering a video game—starts with intrinsic desire, and the path to feeding that desire is often a jumpy experience.

Learning is a series of unpredictable challenges, opportunities, and rewards. This is what makes learning interesting and fun. This is what gets someone hooked. Especially at the start of a journalistic project, learners advance and retreat, progress and regress, and focus on the details, then step back to consider the whole, as illustrated in Figure 3.1.

Our process also takes into consideration that students are choosing to explore complex issues. They may start out identifying problems close to home: *cars on my street go too fast; my sister seems depressed.* These personal concerns can lead to discovering bigger community problems. *Why is traffic worse*

FIGURE 3.1 **Journalistic projects move back and forth from macro to micro concerns, giving them a jumpy feel that mirrors self-directed learning outside of school.**

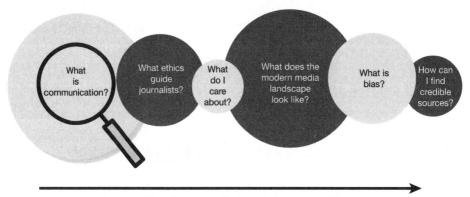

A Journalistic Learning Project Zooms In and Out

Credit: The Journalistic Learning Initiative

around here than in other neighborhoods? How are schools in town supporting middle schoolers' mental health?

The answers are not found with quick Google searches either. Journalistic learning teaches students to query in more meaningful ways. They find out whose job it is to regulate the issue in their community. They identify who's studying it. And they learn who or what organization is trying to help. Their initial vague questions evolve into more refined ones: *Who's in charge of traffic flow and new stop signs in our community? How do they measure traffic? When was the last time the city measured traffic flow in my neighborhood? Have new apps changed traffic patterns here? Have there been official complaints about speeding? What are ways to slow traffic?*

The zoom-in, zoom-out process of journalistic learning prepares students to meaningfully ask important questions about their communities and navigate information outside the classroom on their own. It gives them practice speaking to adults and writing about complicated local problems. In short, it sets them up to be lifelong learners and engaged citizens.

Finding the Class Baseline

Before beginning a journalistic learning project, you may wish to ask students to reflect in writing on what they already know or assume about the news-gathering process. A simple handout with space for students to write can include the following prompts:

- The news is . . .
- What are some ways journalists avoid bias (one-sidedness) in their work?
- What are examples of quantitative details (numbers) you might find in a news article?
- What are examples of qualitative details (description) you might find in a news article?
- What is important to remember when interviewing someone for a news story?
- Describe your confidence level as an online researcher and writer.

These prompts signal to students what they can expect from the project and may help give you a class temperature. If students seem daunted, you can reassure them that by the end of the unit, they will be able to answer all of these questions in a meaningful way. If they seem overly confident or bored, it may be because they haven't considered the complexity of journalism, such as the gray area of bias and whether it's even possible to achieve truly objective reporting—a question that continues to challenge and be debated among professionals. These ideas may not be on students' radars.

The short, written reflection also provides you with information to support learners through each stage of the journalistic process, either by speeding up or slowing down the pace or by providing more practice time. For example, students who feel confident and have experience as online researchers and writers may be able to work quickly during those stages of the project but might need to slow down or see more examples when writing email requests or preparing for interviews.

It's also not uncommon for students to write "I don't know" in this exercise. Because media, news, and information literacies are not yet taught in a systematic or comprehensive way in most schools, there may be significant gaps in understanding and confidence, even in classes of juniors or seniors. That's why we advise teachers to save these baseline papers to return to students at the end of the project so they can add to their original responses. It's a simple but rewarding way for each participant and their teacher to measure growth.

Past and Present: Reading Two Texts to Set the Stage

The purposes of communication are constant: to inform, persuade, assist, sell, connect, teach, entertain, and even to control or harm. What always change are communication methods and tools. These are transforming fast in our particular era and are layered onto most of the communication methods and tools that came before. Consider some ways today's students might communicate an idea:

- Speaking in person
- Telephone
- Writing on paper
- Writing on digital formats: email, texting, public websites, social media
- Photography
- Audio recording
- Video recording

- Live video conferencing
- Virtual reality

One way to show students how communication has changed is to have the class read and discuss articles from different time periods. We like to use two articles from *The New York Times*: "U.S. Bars a Girl's Plea for Russian Pen Pals" (Associated Press, 1960) and "How a Fourth Grader in 1960 Inspired College Students in 2019" (Van Syckle, 2021).

As we outlined in Chapter 1, the first article explains how a class of Oregon fourth-graders during the Cold War era was denied by the U.S. government their request to have Russian pen pals. The second article tells how, 60 years later, a University of Oregon journalism class investigated the outcome of that denial, a project that culminated in an international trip and publication of a book.

The brief texts allow students to contrast communication methods and to reflect on how these changes, both good and bad, might affect ordinary people today. For example, beneficial long-distance friendships can flourish today because it's uncommon and unlikely for democratic governments to prevent private citizens from communicating with each other. On the other hand, disinformation abounds, and it's easier than ever to be insulted or threatened or even to fall victim to online crime.

Comparing historic and contemporary texts gives young people key insight into what a world without borderless, instantaneous communication looked like. From there, your students can begin to see the purpose and power of journalistic learning, introducing them to the communication tools, skills, processes, and formats used by young journalists not much older than themselves who followed a simple question: *Whatever happened to that pen pal project?*

Journalistic Skills for Every Career: Property Inspector

Teachers know that students who develop strong communication skills in interviewing, writing, listening, and speaking tend to experience more success throughout their working lives than those who don't. Many jobs today present the opportunity to use journalistic tools and skills. Property inspectors, for example, observe a property, gather evidence, differentiate serious problems from routine ones, and interpret findings. Inspectors communicate to clients by organizing claims, evidence, and recommendations in digital reports using photographs and video. They use email and speak in person with clients or over the telephone or via video conference.

Introducing Students to Journalism Ethics

Your students may be surprised to learn that most professional journalists in the United States don't get to publish or produce everything they discover and that they can't pay sources for information. The majority of professional news outlets in this country require reporters to follow the Society of Professional Journalists Code of Ethics (SPJ, 2014), a one-page document that describes the foundation of ethical journalism in four principles:

1. Seek Truth and Report It
2. Minimize Harm
3. Act Independently
4. Be Accountable and Transparent

Each of the principles is further explained with a series of "shoulds." For example, listed under Minimize Harm is: "Journalists should balance the public's need for information against potential harm or discomfort. Pursuit of the news is not a license for arrogance or undue intrusiveness."

The idea is that journalists should seek to report the truth, but also should decide if doing so would emotionally harm people. For example, while journalists may take photos or video in the aftermath of a gory vehicle accident or a crime scene, they almost never publish graphic images or describe graphic scenes in detail, out of respect for grieving families.

Unlike many other professions, journalists are not licensed or certified, and there is no law that requires they abide by the industry ethics code. The SPJ recognizes that adhering is aspirational, but most outlets take it seriously. Journalists have been disciplined and even fired, with entire careers lost, for one ethical misstep.

Introducing this one-page code early in the class project can help your students begin to step into the tradition of journalism, to understand how carefully news decisions are monitored and made, and to think critically about the ethics of the news they encounter. It also frames what is allowed in journalism, bringing awareness of boundaries that can influence the later phases of student research, interviewing, and writing.

Research from Kent State University shows that journalism students and news directors agree that "on the job" is the best place to learn journalism (Hanson, 2002). However, middle and high school students usually can't work in a local newsroom. Teachers can compensate by selectively using scenes from film and TV shows, such as HBO's *The Newsroom,* which has proven useful in teaching journalistic ethics due to its portrayal of the industry (Peterlin & Peters, 2019).

Interpreting hypothetical journalism scenarios can also help students experience the complexity and intensity of journalistic decision making. Here's one ethical scenario we've used in classrooms:

> A student reporter is assigned to write a review about a new juice place that opened near campus. She takes a friend along and gets an interview with the store manager, who offers to let each of the students have a smoothie for free and gives the girls coupons for half-priced smoothies to pass out to their friends. *Should the reporter accept the smoothie and coupons? Should she allow her friend to? It's just smoothies; what's the harm?*

Using the SPJ Code of Ethics, students will note the scenario falls under the section "Act Independently," where it states: "Refuse gifts, favors, fees, free travel and special treatment, and avoid political and other outside activities that may compromise integrity or impartiality, or may damage credibility."

Students can imagine themselves in this situation and see that it's clear the reporter should not accept a smoothie from the store manager, but what about her friend? While this is open to interpretation, students might agree that a friend accepting a gift is also a reporter getting special treatment that could compromise the integrity of their reporting—or at least appear to. Perhaps the smoothies are just average, for example, but the reporter views the manager as generous and deserving of an excellent review. It is extremely hard not to want to return a favor, and that in itself creates room for bias.

But what does bias matter when it's just smoothies? To answer, students might ask themselves the purpose of professional restaurant reviews. Does the public want a review created under normal or special circumstances? Clearly, the average reader won't be getting free smoothies just by showing up, so students might conclude that the public wants the reporter to be treated like an ordinary person in order to write an unbiased review so they can anticipate what they will be getting. A teacher might concur and explain that this is why, as a rule, news organizations that employ restaurant reviewers (and movie or theater reviewers) pay for all the reviewer's expenses.

Ask your students to work in small groups to resolve several hypothetical ethical dilemmas. Then have them join with other groups to compare decisions and try to reach consensus. These peer discussions are often rich and high energy, with diverse and interesting outcomes, and teachers can find themselves extending the activity over multiple class periods. The activity also allows your students to develop a working familiarity with the SPJ Code of Ethics and to more easily refer to it at any stage of the project.

One high school English teacher noticed that students today are especially eager to examine society from an ethical perspective:

> My students were very enthusiastic about talking about ethical issues. They see what is going wrong in our society, and they identify so many places where they think that the people in charge aren't being ethical . . . . And as we discussed ethics in journalism, I could see they value this type of consideration. And they're sad that they don't feel like they see this out in the world. So that kind of broke my heart a little bit.

Journalistic Skills for Every Career: Veterinarian

Many professionals have a code of ethics that they are required to follow. Veterinarians, for example, abide by the Principles of Veterinary Medical Ethics, which state that a vet may not perform a surgery that would hide a genetic defect in an animal that is intended to be bred, even if the owner of the pet wants it and is willing to pay extra for it. Veterinarians also use journalistic communication skills, such as active listening and persuasion, to thoughtfully guide pet owners as they face personal moral and financial decisions, such as deciding between euthanasia or expensive medical treatments for an animal that is suffering.

Forming Long-Term Student Groups

Before moving onto the next stage of the project—where your students will choose issues of concern to investigate—take time to think about the two types of groups that students will collaborate in over the course of the project. Figure 3.2 provides an illustration of these two student groups.

The first is a small reporting team, which develops an issue by finding and querying sources and later by writing and editing an article. The second group is a large publishing team, made up of one representative from each reporting team. The larger groups will work on building websites for publication.

Prepare to make two decisions prior to forming student teams:

FIGURE 3.2   **Students collaborate in two different groups over the course of the project. This diagram depicts a class of 34 students.**

Reporting and Publishing Teams

Credit: The Journalistic Learning Initiative

1. How many students should be in each reporting team?

   The ideal size of a reporting team is three students. Groups of four are workable. When students team up in groups of five or more, we have found the work becomes less productive, while groups of two diminish divergent thinking and the collaborative experience. However, there are times when teachers will want to make larger teams:

   - If there are many chronic absences in a class, larger teams allow work to progress even if a few team members are absent.
   - If a class is especially large, bigger reporting teams means fewer groups, and the project can move more quickly through the interview stage. For example, if a teacher has 34 students in groups of 3, they will have 11 teams (see Figure 3.2). This means 11 live interviews over 11 class sessions. With groups of 4, on the other hand, the number of reporting teams drops to 8, requiring 3 fewer class sessions for the interviews.

2. What writing should I require each student to produce?

   There are two options for teachers to consider:

- *Individual writing:* Each student writes their own article, using shared notes from collaborative inquiry. The approach allows teachers to evaluate each student's individual skills and offer personalized feedback and grades. The downside is that it can be difficult for students to transition from collaborating and sharing resources to independently writing an article.
- *Collaborative writing*: Students divide an article into segments. One student writes the beginning, another the middle, and a third the ending. This approach tends to raise group motivation and effort because each student is accountable to their group and collectively responsible for the whole piece. The downside is that one-third of an article may not be a substantial amount of writing for a lengthy project, and it may be more difficult to assess individual student writing progress.

Leveraging Student Concerns into Meaningful Research Topics

We all have gripes, and nobody is a stranger to complaining, venting, or ranting about their individual experience as a human in the 21st century. We've also been affected in recent years by a growing sense of collective anxiety about serious existential issues—climate change, democratic backsliding, pandemics, worsening mental health, economic downturns—that may lead to apathy or even nihilism. Instructors can leverage student concerns into project topics by helping young people connect their personal worries to their community.

Indirectly, journalistic learning can be an antidote for apathy, challenging it in a couple of ways. First, by working with others who care about the same issue, students can see they are not alone in their frustration or concern. Second, students learn that adults are not just standing by; some are working quite purposefully, sometimes just outside of public awareness, on meaningful issues. This can help build students' trust in their community. Students also become aware that some injustices are systemic and that certain groups of people are impacted more than others, through no fault of their own. This new awareness creates empathy for others.

Ask students to begin to reflect on their concerns by writing them down. *What troubles and annoys you? What seems unfair? What should be fixed? What's something that you notice driving or walking around that makes you sad or angry? What are you worried about for yourself or your family or friends?*

Once students have identified their concerns, ask them to distinguish between events and ongoing issues. For this project, we suggest that students focus on issues, not events, in order to explore future solutions to universal concerns. You may need to directly explain the difference using examples such as in Table 3.1.

TABLE 3.1   **Examples of Events vs. Issues**

Event	Issue
A wildfire that came close to a student's home	Forest management as it relates to increased wildfires in urban settings
A 10-car pile-up in the rain that a student's grandmother narrowly escaped	Roads in need of repair or that lack maintenance or safety signs

We suggest choosing one of two paths to forming the long-term reporting teams:

1. Guide the whole class to generate a list of a dozen or so community issues. Then have students sign up to work with like-minded peers.
2. Or divide the class into small reporting teams first. Have the teams brainstorm their own issues.

Some teachers prefer to let the class form groups organically based on student preference. Others like to strategize for long-term success by creating groups that are balanced in certain ways. For example, one veteran high school English teacher who has successfully taught journalistic learning likes to form groups of three with the following characteristics:

- A strong leader who will ask questions, follow up with their teammates, and initiate getting the interviews
- A quiet worker who likes to get things done and is happy to let someone else take on most of the leadership role
- Someone who needs mentoring

"Having a strong leader and a quiet worker allows for someone who needs help and guidance to fit in the middle," she said. "Hopefully, this individual will follow through and learn a lot from the other two without dragging the group down."

It's likely in the beginning of their brainstorming that your students will generate huge ideas. *Why are some Americans going hungry? How is our town affected by inflation?*

For ideas that are just too big to research, ask students to answer some basic questions to bring the issue into sharper focus. It can help to use the traditional journalistic who, what, where, when, why, and how ("5 Ws and 1 H") question frame. For example, if the issue is food insecurity, students can discuss how they would answer the following:

> **Who** *do we know that is affected by food insecurity?*
> **What** *does food insecurity look like in our town?*
> **Where** *do we see food insecurity in our community?*
> **When** *(what time of year or at what age) does food insecurity most affect people?*
> **Why** *do we care about food insecurity?*
> **How** *do people experiencing food insecurity get help in our town?*

Grappling with these questions may lead students to refine their initial topic to have a local focus: *What are the resources and barriers for people in our community who face food insecurity?*

A high school English teacher we spoke with mid-project said she was at first a little concerned about the broad topic choices, but over time she saw a natural winnowing take place:

> At the beginning, students were starting with these big broad topics, but they have narrowed their focus to something that is manageable and that they will be able to find local people to interview. For example, we have two groups in class that started with homelessness, but they've gone in different directions. Now, one is focusing on the resources available in our town, and the other is focusing on the causes.

Another high school teacher described the personal connection her students had to the issues they ultimately chose to investigate:

> These are real issues that are impacting them. I had a student who picked the topic of homelessness because his brother was stabbed by a homeless person, and he was trying to figure out what motivated that person, like what was going on mentally with him? . . . I had a student who picked the topic of shoplifting because he works at Fred Meyers, and he sees shoplift-

ers every day. So, he's trying to figure out what can be done about it, and he's learning a lot about our real-life system.

Adjusting the Project for Students Who Need It

You may find that students who are younger, who are emerging English learners, or who have learning differences need the scope and depth of the project adjusted. This can be done by asking students to focus on a person who is connected to an issue of concern.

For the topic of food insecurity, for example, the inquiry's scope could be changed to: *Who is one person helping people with food insecurity in my community?* Students can ask about the person's career path, their daily responsibilities, their successes and failures, and what would make their job easier. The inquiry and writing process is nearly the same, but the complexity of the topic is reduced.

We recommend not allowing groups to choose the same topic due to the difficulty in finding local sources and to deter unnecessary student competition. We also advise groups to hold a backup issue in reserve in case they decide their first choice has too many barriers.

Helping Students Discuss Uncomfortable Topics

Some of your students may wish to work on issues that are uncomfortable to talk about. In the secondary language arts classroom, as in history and social studies, student discourse around uncomfortable topics is routine.

Whether it's analyzing how an author depicts a character's loss of innocence due to war or examining a character's death or suicide, English teachers are accustomed to leading students into and through troubling, even painful, conversations. Supporting students as they grow to understand and accept the many difficulties and wonders of being human is one of the privileges of the job.

Outside of fiction, poetry, and history, many teachers also find meaningful ways to read about and discuss current events so that students gain practice with reading informative texts and understand that the themes of beauty and suffering are present today too.

In recent years, however, classroom discourse has become its own uncomfortable topic in some communities, with dozens of states seeking to enact laws meant to restrict how public school teachers and students discuss the nation's past and present.

Some of the legislation proposes restricting topics of racism and bias by banning instruction of Critical Race Theory, an academic framework used in some university-level courses to examine the policies and laws that perpetuate systemic racism.

Other states are working to expand class discourse on racism and bias by mandating new ethnic studies courses or by developing learning standards around cultural competency, diversity, equity, and inclusion. They seek to encourage and develop cultural understanding of how different groups have struggled and worked together.

Teaching about racism is particularly divisive today. A 2022 "Mood of the Nation" survey of 1,200 American adults conducted by APM Research Lab and the McCourtney Institute for Democracy at Penn State University found:

- 49% say schools have a responsibility to teach students the ongoing effects of slavery and racism in America
- 41% believe schools should only teach the history of slavery and racism—not race relations today
- 10% say schools have no responsibility to teach students the history of slavery and racism in the United States

Teachers are concerned, with 37% of 2,000 teachers saying they will leave the profession if K–12 censorship laws reach their school, according to a survey published in early 2022 by the nonprofit Stand for Children and SurveyUSA, an independent research firm.

Controversy over what students learn in school is not new. There is a history of challenges to the topics that are taught in U.S. public schools. In the 1840s and 1850s, politicians and prominent citizens of southern states advocated for home schooling to keep northern teachers (and their ideas about abolition) out of southern schools (Groen, 2013).

In 1925, John Thomas Scopes was tried for violating the Tennessee law that made teaching human evolution in a public school illegal. After the *Brown v. Board of Education of Topeka* ruling in 1954, private schools known as segregation academies began forming in the southern United States to circumvent integrated schooling (Walder & Cleveland, 1971).

In 1961, anxiety around the Cold War and multiculturalism sparked controversy over social studies in Texas (Kownslar, 2019). Public schools saw dramatic increases in complaints about textbooks and libraries resulting in censorship in the 1980s (Hechinger, 1984). And in 2014, students in Colorado walked out of school to protest censorship in curriculum revisions (Healy, 2014). More recently, states have enacted controversial laws that limit what can be taught in schools, such as sexual orientation and gender identity in Florida (Mazzei, 2022) and race and racism in Texas (Garcia, 2021).

We highlight these ongoing challenges in education not to dismiss the current landscape but instead to anchor in historical context what teachers are now facing and to acknowledge the difficult but deeply valuable work of teachers in promoting diverse, critical thought among students, even in the face of social, cultural, political, and legal challenges.

We believe educators have a moral obligation to support learners in understanding their own concerns through their inquiry and discussion. With all that's going on in the contemporary educational climate, with changing tides of public and parent opinion, the journalistic approach offers a way forward.

Of course, teachers can and should set parameters on how discourse originates in their classrooms and how it takes place throughout the project, including helping to moderate student discussions without giving away their own perspectives and opinions.

One 11th-grade English teacher who teaches journalistic learning explains his approach to tough conversations:

> Trust and respect are the hallmarks of an inclusive classroom, but that trust can be easily eroded if the classroom teacher demonstrates obvious bias from the outset. I do have very strong opinions, of course, but I rarely let those opinions out. Instead, I try to show students the value of civil discourse by setting ground rules for discussion and debate that are rooted in kindness and empathy. We do not all have to agree, but every one of my students knows that there is no space in our conversations for hate or discrimination. By keeping my opinions to myself, I allow my students the freedom to express themselves without worrying that I will judge them or be disappointed.

A 10th-grade teacher requires students to back up their opinions with facts:

> In order for students to feel respect for their peers and the class culture, I ask that when expressing ideas that might make people uncomfortable, that they be grounded in the text we are reading, or research that has been done from a reasonable source. This tends to curb the "off the cuff" comments.

Sadly, teachers report that students have become more hesitant to offer opinions in class, a self-censorship trend that has emerged in recent years. For some young people, remaining quiet during class discussions became an ingrained habit during the COVID-19 pandemic's learn-at-home stages, where hour after hour of video conferencing limited peer discourse in profound ways.

Other students worry they may be censored or socially "canceled" for speaking their opinions in class, perhaps a reflection of how readily speech and opinions can be attacked on social media. This reality makes speaking up among peers seem especially risky, as if there is no real margin to learn from mistakes or no grace to change one's mind.

A ninth-grade teacher explains what she sees in her classes today:

> As our world gets more extreme and divided, it has trickled down to students. I have seen more inflexible students who don't want to listen to the other side and who veer towards being a bit disrespectful. So far it has been manageable, but I am worried.
>
> For the most part, students are respectful, but I have had one or two who struggle with perspective-taking and are so vehement and inflexible in their opinions that they make the open exchange of ideas difficult. This year, after the pandemic and with so much polarization in our communities, students have openly expressed that they don't want to share viewpoints for fear of offending someone or having their viewpoints stigmatized.

Journalistic learning can help build a culture of trust by including low-risk thinking activities such as reflective writing prior to group discussion, which provides more processing time for students to figure out how to say what they want to say.

As we will explore in the next chapter, journalistic learning decenters student opinion right from the start by requiring learners to research facts, create fair questions, and learn directly from community experts. This process typically leads to high-quality discussion, with students growing in their confidence to assert what they've discovered.

Connecting Students to Their Local News

Once students have worked in reporting teams to choose an issue they care about, it's a good idea to give them a class period to search for past coverage in local media outlets, including community or regional newspapers, local TV broadcasts, and radio websites.

This quick exploration of the local news landscape may feel somewhat cursory since students have not yet developed a focused line of inquiry, but this is purposeful. There are three goals for the mini exploration at this early stage:

1. Students learn who is producing quality local news.
2. They experience searching and navigating diverse digital news sites.
3. They develop an impression of the local history and breadth of their selected issue.

Create a list of local outlets in advance and model how to use a media outlet's internal search tool by doing a hypothetical search. Be sure to show how to handle unproductive searches in real time by redefining key search terms.

Students can take some notes at this stage, but if the coverage of their chosen issue is extensive, they should merely skim the news to try to grasp its scope and depth.

Paywalls and News Deserts: Overcoming Barriers to Local News Research

One barrier you and your students will almost certainly face is news paywalls. While frustrating, students must learn that free information is not always high-quality information.

Producing accurate, timely information, at the local (or any) level is expensive, and we believe the people who work in journalism deserve to be well-compensated for their labor. We also believe that students who experience high-quality local news at a young age are likely to value journalism and subscribe to a community outlet when they grow up. We encourage news editors to work with educators to create opportunities for student access.

Because purchasing a subscription for every student is probably prohibitive at most schools, we recommend you contact local publishers in advance to ask for free or low-cost entry to digital news websites for the length of the project, typically three months. Supportive librarians or media specialists on campus may be able to help make these requests. A template of a letter is provided as example A.1 in Appendix A.

A second barrier classes may face is the absence or sparsity of quality local news. The United States has more than 1,300 news deserts, with more than two-thirds of the country's 3,143 counties no longer having a daily newspaper (Abernathy, 2018). Even more troubling, 171 counties—totaling 3.2 million residents—have no newspaper at all.

Students and their families are affected by this issue. One high school teacher explained that her community's lack of newspapers and broadcast news stations means most community members get their news through social media.

We believe it's worth teaching students why their town may not have a newspaper anymore or why their local newspaper now may seem weak compared to 10 or more years ago. One reason is that news production has traditionally secured most of its funding from advertising, not sub-scriptions or public funding, both of which served to supplement rather than sustain the budget. At the beginning of this century, as ads moved to other places—search engines and social media mostly—so did the revenue. Local newspapers struggled financially with this shift, which continues, and many local owners decided to sell and get out of the news business altogether.

You might wish to have students read the October 2021 article "What We Lost When Gannett Came to Town" in *The Atlantic*, in which Elaine Godfrey poignantly describes the decline of *The Hawk Eye* newspaper, founded in 1887, in Burlington, Iowa. She details how *The Hawk Eye* collapse started in 2016 when it was purchased by New York City publishing company GateHouse, which is run by an investment firm. Shortly after, GateHouse bought Gannett Company, which publishes *USA Today* and about 100 daily and 1,000 weekly American newspapers.

Over five years, the 100-member staff at *The Hawk Eye* was downsized to about a dozen employees today, with even fewer reporters. The ability of a handful of professional journalists to comprehensively cover the Burlington community is now impossible, Godfrey explains.

For her, it's also personal; this was the 200-year-old paper she grew up with and that her family still reads. She writes touchingly about the loss of coverage of quotidian happenings such as the annual teddy bear picnic, the new swimming pool design at the recreation center, and the tractor games at the fair. Losing these stories represents to her the loss of community and connection.

A third barrier to finding quality news is the emergence of local parti-san publications that look and feel like community publishers but that do not approach news with standards, professional ethics, fairness, or neutrality.

While running a full-fledged newsroom is expensive, operating a one-person digital news website is practically free.

We advise teachers to research their news landscape in advance, before students happen upon these types of publications, to be prepared to explain why these are not appropriate for the project. One way to familiarize yourself with the local news scene is to look up your county on the website "The Expanding News Desert," curated by the Hussman School of Journalism at the University of North Carolina. The site offers maps and statistics and can be accessed at https://www.usnewsdeserts.com.

Writing What They Know (So Far)

Once students have dipped into local research, it's helpful—if not a bit counterintuitive—to have them try to write about their selected issue prior to formal research. A "write what you know" exercise can serve as a loose pre-draft and as the basis of a story pitch. This writing is a starting place for students to recognize their knowledge gaps and to think about the types of questions they will want to ask people during the interview stage.

In this exercise, have your students set aside any notes they've gathered and free write everything they know about their chosen issue in about 10 to 15 minutes with no other prompts. This may be stressful for some students as they realize how few facts they know and how big the issue is. They may lose confidence in their ability to pursue the issue. This is normal and usually temporary. Journalists almost always feel this way at the start of a major inquiry. Later in the project, students are taught refined inquiry and writing practices to help them achieve their goals step by step. For now, it's enough to summarize what they think they know so far.

After free writing, students can reflect together with their reporting teams on two questions:

1. After reading about this issue, do you think it is more or less important than before you looked into it? Why?
2. Do you still care about this issue enough to research it, or do you want to change it? Why?

This discussion may lead reporting teams to switch to a backup issue. Changing topics at this point is fine. It's better for students to release an idea now if it no longer resonates than to push forward with it in hopes that it will somehow respark interest. Some reporting teams may need to spend another class period diving back into local news to learn about their second-choice issue before proceeding.

Drafting a Story Pitch

Pitch sheets can be useful at this stage. Because newsroom resources are limited, professional journalists often talk with their editors about story ideas to get the go-ahead before beginning an intensive inquiry. Pitching an idea in its nascent form helps students understand whether they know enough to begin more complex research. It also demonstrates that they have developed some interesting questions and can anticipate why other people might care about the issue. And it helps identify gaps in understanding.

The journalist's pitch sheet should have places for students to make notes on the following:

1. *Stakeholders:* What groups of people (or other living creatures) are affected by this issue?

2. *Sources:* Who are the local experts on this issue? List types of experts from the different stakeholder groups who could be interviewed to share what they know. You don't need names yet, just categories of people. If you have specific names, go ahead and write them down. An expert can be someone with training, academic credentials, or deep experience with the issue.

3. *Questions:* What do you want to find out about this issue? Write your ideas as questions starting with who, what, where, when, why, and how.

4. *Articles:* What reporting has already been done on this issue? Searching online news, read several news articles about your top issue. Choose two that offer helpful facts or people you might interview. For both articles, note:
   a. Name of news outlet
   b. Date of article
   c. Headline
   d. Most interesting quotes

5. *Additional details:* List a few new facts that were not in your summary.

6. *Write a pitch:* In four or five sentences, write a pitch to an imaginary

editor. Pretend you are asking to report on this issue, and you need to prove it is worthy of the outlet's time and money. You hope to show the editor two things:

    a. You know enough about the issue to begin the next phase of research and interviewing.

    b. Your questions are ones that others will care about and you can probably find answers to.

A pitch might read like this:

> Over the last five years, food insecurity in the United States has increased. We would like to know if this trend is also happening in our community and what options there are for people to not go hungry if they can't afford to eat well. School-age children are served free meals at school, and even during the pandemic families picked up food prepared by school kitchens. But what happens to children younger than school age? What happens to young adults over 18? We'd like to interview a local food bank manager and/or a person who has experienced food insecurity here to get their insights and experience.

The pitch sheet can be augmented and revised as the project continues into the inquiry stage. You might want to ask students to read their pitches to peers, other teachers, or to you, which allows them to practice speaking and provides them with immediate feedback on their proposals.

Journalistic Skills for Every Career: Coffee Shop Entrepreneur

Small businesses are pitched and launched in the United States every day by individuals who use online inquiry to fuel their dreams. One young Pennsylvania entrepreneur who successfully opened a coffee shop with no experience or formal business training told us that he "liked to go four pages into online research to try to find something that might be different and at the heart of stuff." There were all kinds of things to be aware of that he didn't have answers to at first: how to build a business plan, what regulations to follow, how to prepare the best latte. He also reached out to people in the area and sat down with them to ask questions so he could "keep peeling the onion back" to find the exact information he needed. Discovering what you don't know is a meta-cognitive practice that can make the difference between adequate and inadequate preparation, and ultimately between business success and failure.

CHAPTER 4

Sifting Through the Noise

"Gen Z does not want to put their phones away."
—10th-Grade World Literature Teacher

STUDENTS TODAY SWIM IN a vast media ocean, and like the proverbial fish that wonders aloud what water is because it's never known any other environment, it can be especially hard for them to understand the forces bobbing and weaving across their screens. Digital news, including bits and scraps of out-of-context claims and misinformation, flows across their devices, buffeted by memes, video clips, games, texts, music, photos, ads, social media posts, and more.

Digital media is ubiquitous for middle and high school students; 84% of American teens own a smartphone, and they spend an average of seven hours a day on screen entertainment, according to a recent study by Common Sense Media (Rideout & Robb, 2019). The evolution of media in our lifetimes alone has been exponential, and the content available to children, much of it free, has exploded.

It's not easy for any of us to attend to wave after wave of data. It takes sustained effort to interpret all the underlying motives that feed possibility and pitfall into our six- by three-inch flickering screens, which are always, always within reach. Information. Communication. Connection. Transaction. Temptation. Manipulation. Confusion. Division. It's all here.

As educators, we love digital media and believe in its power to change lives by telling meaningful stories and empowering people who historically have not been given voice and agency. But while much about the modern media landscape is beneficial, inspiring, and fun, young people need to be able to navigate the flip side, finding their way around and through the bad stuff.

An 11th-grade teacher explains:

I really believe that it's more important than ever to learn about how bias can lead to, you know, just bad news. We're surrounded by lots of media that are so biased in their reporting. Kids are seeing this. Adults are seeing this.

While your students may be eager to dig into the research phase of their project and start contacting experts in their community, we encourage you to take time at this stage to help them learn about the systems and structures of the modern media landscape, guiding them to be skeptical, not cynical, as they analyze online content.

One 10th-grade English teacher who launched a journalistic learning project in spring 2022 saw firsthand how her teenage students brought preexisting biases about the media into her classroom.

"A lot of them had a very negative view of the media," she said. "They felt the media was this one big overarching thing, this big entity, and now they're starting to understand that there are many, many facets to media. It's changing their view."

In this chapter, we outline activities that will help your students spot sophisticated digital advertising practices that blur news and sales content. We introduce a four-step strategy called SIFT, used at the college level and adapted here for middle and high school, that can empower your class to scrutinize claims and sources. And we offer practical approaches to helping young people examine and interpret degrees of bias in the news.

Surveying the Media Scene

To help students step back and consider the scope of the mass media landscape, you might have them start with a simple categorization activity. Working as a class, guide them to develop a list of the types of media that exist today, for example, video games, podcasts, radio shows, books, email, websites, social media, magazines, music, comics, news, advertising, movies, sitcoms, blogs/vlogs, newsletters, and memes.

Then have students sort the media types they brainstormed into common delivery methods:

- *Print:* newspapers, magazines, comics, books, ads, informational brochures or postcards
- *Broadcast:* television news, radio news, music, movies, sitcoms, ads
- *Digital:* website news, social media news, video games, social media, movies, blogs/vlogs, podcasts, email

This simple analysis doesn't take long and can help students form a basic mental schema of the media landscape. It's a great way to talk with them about how the media ecosystems have changed over the last few decades. How many of the media types simply didn't exist when you were their age, for example? How have new delivery methods changed news consumption for this generation? You might help them notice how digital news—like the kind they will be writing—competes with many forms of digital entertainment for user attention. What obstacles will that present in terms of getting readers to pay attention to their work?

It's also helpful to discuss the types of news publications that make up the industry, including:

- *Geographically organized publications:* hyperlocal, local, regional, state, national, international publications
- *Genre publications:* politics, sports, celebrities, music, etc.

Where will their articles fit once published?

Asking students to imagine and discuss generational shifts can be interesting, too:

- Which news do you care about most these days?
- Which news do you think your parents or grandparents care about most?

Compared to their parents or grandparents, students might identify themselves as belonging to specialized news audiences, say high school sports or K-pop or LGBTQ rights, rather than to a general news audience. Because no single news outlet can comprehensively serve all these audiences, niche outlets arise and flourish by sharing content across diverse social media, which is one way things can get so confusing.

How Are Your Students Getting Their News?

While print newspapers may have been a staple of family life for some of us growing up, print is clearly on the decline. It is estimated that daily print newspaper subscriptions in the United States have dropped by 61%, from a peak of 62.8 million in 1987 to just 24.3 million in 2020 (Pew Research Center, 2021).

Many news outlets offer a hybrid model. The biggest may offer print plus sophisticated websites with digital articles, photos, videos, live streams, blogs, podcasts, comics, games, and interactive curated comments. Many smaller outlets cut operating costs by canceling Saturday print editions or ending print runs altogether to focus entirely on digital news.

Unlike their parents or grandparents, teens today rarely watch TV news. In fact, they watch very little television at all, just 25 minutes of TV programming as it airs per day on average, according to Common Sense Media (Rideout & Robb, 2019). Instead, they've developed omnivorous news tendencies. A study by Project Information Literacy, a national research institute that studies information practices in the digital age, found in 2019 that two-thirds of surveyed undergraduates received news daily from five pathways (Head et al., 2020). These include:

- social media—72%
- peer discussion, either face-to-face or online—48%
- online newspaper sites—32%
- classroom discussion with professors—23%
- curated feeds (Apple News, etc.)—32%

Only 15% of the surveyed students reported watching TV news daily, about the same number as reported listening to daily radio news.

It's quite possible the middle or high school students on your rosters may be unaware of what constitutes news, and therefore may not consider themselves even to be news consumers. Sure, they might follow pop culture trends or check sports scores or share breaking current events through conversation, but they may not identify these activities as news habits.

We encourage you to survey your students about how they get daily news. A simple questionnaire can help you understand how different their consumption habits may be from your own, and it can help them visualize the various information pathways they and their peers rely on. Teachers can create a simple anonymous digital survey that asks:

1. In the last week, how often did you read, watch, or listen to the news?
    a. Every day
    b. About half the days
    c. Once or twice

     d. Never
2. In the last week, how did you get news? (Check all that apply):
     a. Print paper or magazine
     b. Digital news website
     c. Television
     d. YouTube
     e. Radio
     f. Social media
     g. Text message
     h. Email
     i. Word of mouth (parents, friends)
3. In the last week, if you got news from social media, where did you get it? (Check all that apply):
     a. TikTok
     b. Snapchat
     c. Instagram
     d. Facebook
     e. YouTube
     f. Reddit
     g. LinkedIn
     h. Pinterest
     i. Tumblr
     j. Other

This type of survey creates rich discussion opportunities that build naturally to an essential question, perhaps the question of our era: *How do we know what news is true?*

A Note on Vocabulary: Use of "The Media"

"Media" is a collective noun. In the context of news, a "medium" is a single publication or program, while "media" is the plural form and indicates many publications or programs. To be grammatically correct, we should say: "The media *are* the focus of our class today." However, people in the United States more commonly use a singular verb, "The media *is* the focus of our class today."

The Modern Language Association (2020) cites the Merriam-Webster dictionary, which states that "media" can be treated as singular or plural when referred to mass media. So, students may choose either style for their writing, if they are consistent. For this book, we are using the more common singular verb: "The media *is* . . . " Teachers might want to present this grammatical nuance to students to help them understand that despite the singular verb, the term "the media" comprises multiple entities and is not monolithic. Pausing discussion and helping students to clarify their language can be especially valuable if students talk about "the media" in an all-encompassing way such as, "The media is ignoring this issue we care about!" when they only mean social media or television news. Being more specific in their thinking and language can help students think about the media they use in more subtle ways.

Countering Conspiratorial Thinking About "The Media"

As you may remember from civics class, journalism is known as "the fourth estate," serving as the unofficial fourth pillar of U.S. representative democracy. The free press is a watchdog for the people, checking the powers of the legislative, executive, and judicial branches of government by shining light on matters some might prefer to be transacted in the dark. Journalism plays a critical role in allowing citizens to understand and engage with local, regional, and state governmental bodies, from school boards and city councils to statehouses.

Before the emergence of the information free-for-all that is the internet, gatekeepers once controlled the flow of news and information. Publishers paid professional journalists, researchers, and editors to gather, verify, and edit information before publishing. Although they dealt with news flashes and breaking news, too, this process, along with the expense of printing or broadcasting, restricted news in the past to both a slower pace and a higher burden of proof than what is experienced in the age of digital news and information.

Today, gatekeepers still exist on the web and elsewhere, but they face increasing competition from ordinary citizens who hit the "share" button with little forethought and from algorithms that amplify those shares exponentially. Gatekeepers also are overwhelmed by independent journalists or so-called news organizations that don't prioritize accuracy and that excuse sloppy or sensational reporting in order to be first with a hot take.

We've all probably learned some hard lessons about taking information at face value; however, these days healthy skepticism has devolved into wide cynicism about the journalism profession. Perhaps it's exhaustion from doom scrolling through social media while trying with limited success to be the arbiter of what is true and useful amid so many false claims and cloaked sales pitches. Maybe it's the rise of rhetoric from partisan news outlets. Or possibly it's yet another sign of the struggles facing local journalism—an institution that once helped build and strengthen community ties but now is barely keeping up.

Politicians who weaponize the term "the media" for political gain have not helped, but they are not exactly a new phenomenon either. A 1972 Gallup survey found that 68% of Americans had a "great deal or fair amount of trust" in the media to report the news fully, accurately, and fairly (Brenan, 2020). That was when the news media was referred to as "the press." Journalist Martin F. Nolan (2005) found that the term changed because of President Richard Nixon's dislike of journalists. His wish to undermine reporters sparked a subtle semantic transition from "the press" to "the media" and then became an all-encompassing journalism-bashing moniker.

Four decades later, distrust in the media was exacerbated during the Trump administration. In fact, Trump said on his first day in office that he had "a running war with the media" and that journalists were "the most dishonest human beings on Earth" (Glaser, 2017). Then he doubled down and labeled the press "enemies of the people" (Smith, 2019). The rhetoric was effective, with American trust in the media to report the news "fully, accurately and fairly" dipping to a record low of 32% in 2016, according to Gallup (Swift, 2016). When powerful people say over and over that the media is lying to you or the media has an agenda, collective trust in a free press is degraded, which contributes to conspiratorial thinking.

Of course, it's entirely fair to acknowledge that journalists sometimes suffer from following routine reporting practices that don't lead to presenting a diversity of voices, experiences, or opinions. For example, reporters sometimes rely on easily accessed officials and policy makers for fast interviews instead of digging deeper to amplify the voices of those most affected by decisions.

Journalists can also be guilty of creating their own echo chambers by too closely following the lead of their peers who break news. These practices—sometimes lazy, sometimes due to a lack of resources, imagination, or experience—can cause rural community members to feel disconnected from city dwellers. And they can lead people in communities of color to criticize mainstream media for being insensitive and disregarding their concerns.

The public today is somewhat suspicious of a master agenda being played out behind their backs. The partisan gap is particularly striking, with 73% of Democrats in 2020 stating they have "a great detail or fair amount" of trust in the media, but only 10% of Republicans claiming to (Brenan, 2020). This is the invisible chasm that teachers face every day as they look out at their students: some are being raised in families that implicitly trust journalists; others are not.

The journalistic learning approach pushes back on broad cynicism about the media by helping students examine and infer how unlikely it would be for competing news outlets across various formats and platforms to coordinate common talking points in order to produce a coordinated so-called media agenda or a media lie.

To start such an examination, you might consider asking students the simple question: *Who controls the news?* See what preconceptions exist. One answer (and you really must clear this up if it arises as a point of confusion) is not the government. The First Amendment of the U.S. Constitution—just 45 words long!—creates room for an independent press that can report on public concerns without fear of government oversight or censorship. It states:

> Congress shall make no law respecting an establishment of religion, or prohibiting the free exercise thereof; or abridging the freedom of speech, or of the press; or the right of the people peaceably to assemble, and to petition the Government for a redress of grievances.

Simply put, the government, whether it's the president of the United States or the head of a local transportation department, is constitutionally prohibited from censoring or organizing or interfering with the independent press. Journalists are allowed to freely question and report on past, present, or future government actions, with few exceptions, mostly having to do with national security.

Take time to analyze the words of the First Amendment as a class to help students understand or absorb the meaning.

Who Controls the News?

Since the government doesn't control the news or set an agenda, students may be wondering who does. It can be helpful to briefly explain to students how journalism is funded. News ownership can be broadly divided into for-profit and nonprofit structures.

For-profit news outlets might be funded by:

- *an individual:* for example, billionaire bio scientist Patrick Soon-Shiong owns *The Los Angeles Times*
- *a family:* for example, *The Keene Sentinel* in Keene, New Hampshire, has been an independent, family-owned publication since 1799
- *a corporation that is publicly traded:* for example, The New York Times Company owns *The New York Times*
- *a parent company that owns multiple news outlets:* for example, Disney owns ABC News and ESPN

Nonprofit news outlets do not have shareholders and are not commercially driven entities. They reinvest revenues back into the organization and might be funded by:

- *a nonprofit entity:* for example, the Lenfest Institute, a subsidiary of the Philadelphia Foundations, owns *The Philadelphia Inquirer*
- *tax-deductible donations:* for example, *The Breckenridge Texan* is a certified nonprofit news organization sponsored by the Institute for Nonprofit News
- *direct government subsidies:* for example, the Public Broadcasting Service
- *community member contributions:* for example, National Public Radio

Students should understand that many, if not most, news outlets compete against each other for ad dollars, subscribers, and viewer or reader attention. *The Washington Post* and *The New York Times* are fierce competitors on national and international news, for example. While their journalists may cover the same stories, they don't collaborate—they try to beat each other by being first, most thorough, and most accurate or by showing a different angle in their stories.

You might ask students to briefly examine their local media to see how community news outlets fit. Ask them to use Wikipedia to do a quick dive into their regional news outlets. Reporting teams can choose one outlet in the community and present the following to their classmates:

- Year publication or program was founded
- Last year it was sold
- Delivery formats it uses
- Geographical audience it serves

- Estimated number of subscribers
- Business model or ownership structure
- An interesting fact

Between First Amendment protections against government influence and the market realities, students should come to learn that individual professional journalists have little incentive or ability to conspire, coordinate, or organize a vast media lie across competing outlets and platforms. At the same time, because of increasing media consolidation and concentration, trends and patterns can emerge across news media broadly in the kinds of stories that are covered, the amount of coverage they get, and the angle of the coverage.

Helping Students Distinguish News from Opinion and Ads

Back when newspapers dominated the way people engaged with media, the line between news and opinion was more obvious. Front page stories in major professional newspapers tended to be factual and devoid of hyperbole or conjecture. Front page stories in newspapers with a political bias or a focus on scandals (often called tabloids) trumpeted their point of view. Generally, the editorial page was where management would take a stance on any issue, where columnists had license to assert their personal perspectives, and where letters from readers were published.

Today, the blurring of online news, opinion, and advertising makes it hard even for adults to distinguish a sales pitch or a hot take from cold, hard facts. A haze—an informational smog, if you will—has emerged over decades. Once upon a time in broadcast news, for example, the anchor desk was a symbol of news authority. Then came the 1990s, an era when informational television took a tabloid turn with the sudden proliferation of ratings-winning, news-like shows, including *A Current Affair, Hard Copy,* and *Inside Edition,* all of which featured an anchor desk. Often scheduled adjacent to traditional news, these programs led to an era of infotainment, and audiences began to find it more difficult to discern legitimate news from sensationalism.

Simultaneously, the prime time cable news industry entered an era of panelization since casting pundits to engage in heated debates proved far less costly than going out and covering news from the street. Then came the superstars of prime-time cable television, commentators such as Rachel Maddow and Tucker Carlson, who cultivated significant audiences that generally agree with their political takes. Opinionated lecturing about the day's news stirs our emotions, hooking us on cycles of outrage. This pleases advertisers and increases corporate profits but does little to advance a holistic understanding of the facts.

Navigating the online world of news, opinion, and advertising is probably a challenge for most of your students, who during their journalistic research likely will come across the full spectrum of persuasive content that exists side by side with news. It's quite possible they have never been asked to examine—or even notice—the difference.

But don't young people have an internal sense of how to navigate online information? After all, an online world is the only world they've ever known, so they should be savvy enough to tell the difference between sponsored content and hard news, right?

Not so, according to research from the Stanford History Education Group (SHEG). Led by Sam Wineberg, the group studies students' online reasoning and information evaluation skills. A 2021 SHEG study of 3,446 students reported that two-thirds of U.S. high schoolers cannot differentiate between news and ads online (Breakstone et al., 2021). Half of the students in the study believed an unverified Facebook video was a source of credible evidence. What's more, less than 2% of the students used effective and reliable techniques to evaluate website credibility.

This study, and others like it, paint a discouraging picture: the same generation that lives and breathes the digital world like fish in water is ill-prepared to swim. Students don't know how to disentangle truth from fiction online.

So, what can teachers do? For starters, any discussion about online information should include a conversation about motives. For language arts teachers, this is similar to talking about an author's intention in a story, speech, or letter. Communication takes effort, and effort is always motivated. Someone wants something.

Students should learn that on any given news webpage or social media stream they can typically find evidence of four motives (sometimes overlapping):

To inform
To persuade
To sell
To entertain

Using examples from a digital newspaper homepage, point out and discuss how to recognize:

- *Opinion:* an article that explicitly reflects the viewpoint of the author and is usually housed in the Opinion or Editorial section of a news site
- *Editorial:* an article, collectively written, that explicitly reflects the viewpoint of a publication's editorial board
- *Op-Ed:* an article that explicitly reflects the viewpoint of the author, submitted by a member of the community, not written by publication staff (the term stands for "opposite the editorial page," which is where you will find them in print publications)
- *Column:* typically, a more personal essay, written regularly (once a week, etc.) by a member of the publication staff

Then show examples of:

- *Traditional advertising*: images or text that obviously promote a product, service, or event
- *Native advertising (sponsored content and paid partnerships)*: articles, videos and podcasts created for a brand to sell a product

In native advertising, brands pay news outlets to publish content in a way that looks very close if not identical to the news. For example, a persuasive article with a newsy headline may appear in a list of legitimate news headlines, but it includes a link to a product page where you can make a purchase. Pop culture websites often publish listicles (the portmanteau for articles that use a list format) to share content like "14 Funniest Viral Videos" that are written by or in conjunction with brand or product marketing teams but look nearly identical to their staff-written listicles.

Make students aware of the traditional divide between editorial and sales in journalism (a divide that is becoming narrower year by year). In the past, editorial departments were strictly for the journalists who produced news, opinion, sports, business, technology, features, entertainment, and opinion content.

In the 1800s, for example, the *Chicago Tribune* used two elevators and distinct office areas to deliberately separate editorial and business employees (Birnbauer, 2018). The business side was for the sales teams and was where ads and subscriptions were managed. The journalists were discouraged from even casually talking to the folks in sales, so nobody could claim that a publisher's business interests influenced the journalistic mission to deliver the truth.

This tradition has faded. In fact, some larger news outlets now have in-house digital advertising studios that track and use readership metrics from their own editorial content to develop custom sales content for outside brands. You can now find beautifully researched and designed feature articles that look and read just like news and that often run alongside news. *The New York Times*, for example, has an in-house studio called T Brand, with its own website that states:

> We create stories that live across *The New York Times* Advertising platform and guarantee reach via a mix of Times channels. This work can be crafted to continue on in a brand's social channels, as out of home placements, or anywhere your story should be told for the best impact. (*Method*, n.d.)

Typically, this type of non-journalism content carries a clear label indicating it is native advertising. There might be a note at the top of the webpage that reads "paid post" or "sponsored content." Or a byline will indicate a non-journalism affiliation. However, when such content is distributed on social media, readers may not see the label prior to clicking. They assume they're going to a legitimate news article, when in fact it is a newsy advertisement. It's easy to see why fewer than 1 in 10 adults in the United States can recognize native advertising (Amazeen & Wojdynski, 2019).

There are few guardrails in place to help news consumers who are confused by sophisticated or out-of-context "advertorials." Unlike in the professional journalism industry, advertising ethics have never really existed to guide the practice in a meaningful way.

The Federal Trade Commission, an independent federal agency that tries to protect consumers from unfair practices by regulating deceptive advertising, has stepped up to try to help monitor the shifting landscape:

> In digital media, a publisher, or an authorized third party, can easily and inexpensively format an ad so it matches the style and layout of the content into which it is integrated in ways not previously available in traditional media. The effect is to mask the signals consumers customarily have relied upon to recognize an advertising or promotional message.
>
> At the same time, the business models of many publishers also have undergone significant change, as, increasingly, consumers are able to skip or block digital ads while watching digitized programming or browsing publisher content. Consequently, many publishers have begun to offer advertisers formats and techniques that are closely integrated with and

less distinguishable from regular content so that they can capture the attention and clicks of ad-avoiding consumers. (Federal Trade Commission, 2015, p. 2)

Giving students time to practice distinguishing news from opinion and sales content can go a long way to helping them gain agency in such a confusing online space.

One effective way to do this is to simply have them pull up a news website and ask them to identify and count the number of ads, both traditional and native, among the news articles and opinion pieces. See if they can do it without clicking into the content, so that they can learn to spot the difference with as little time and effort as possible.

A half hour of this analysis can be clarifying and can build their overall sense of the online news landscape, especially if students present what they find across different sites.

(Note: Your school's internet filter may automatically block ads, so you might need to prepare screenshots of some home pages in advance for students to review.)

Introducing SIFT: Four Steps to Checking Online Information

The foraging habits of young news consumers, the diminished editorial gate-keeping, and the blurring of news and advertising combine to present a significant challenge when it comes to helping students determine the credibility of information. Media technologies are constantly evolving, and media literacy education may still be hit or miss in earlier grades. Bad information and digital noise abound online, including:

- *Misinformation:* false information that spreads because people believe it's true (even though it isn't). This includes information that is out of context, out of date, or misunderstood.
- *Disinformation:* false information that spreads purposely even though it's known to be false (for nefarious purposes). Russian disinformation campaigns surrounding COVID-19 vaccinations and the 2016 election are examples of disinformation.

Some secondary teachers strive to independently find or create activities and resources to address media literacy gaps, while others are mandated to use a specific media literacy curriculum. However, as every teacher knows, using lessons that are holistically detached from course content can make crucial skills seem less relevant or interesting, and what is learned in a tacked on lesson has a tendency not to transfer to everyday practice or long-term memory. As a veteran high school teacher noted:

> Many of my 10th-graders did not have to really navigate internet searches beyond typing something into Google and then taking whatever popped up at the top of Google and counting that as a source. Some didn't even seem to realize that the response in Google was coming from someplace else and (cited the information) as "Google said."

Students learn and remember media literacy strategies best when they are used in pursuit of information that matters to them in the moment, such as while researching a topic of concern or when seeking credible sources to interview, with publication for a real audience just around the corner.

The four-step SIFT process that we are about to introduce fits well at this early stage of your journalistic learning project. The acronym helps students remember to Stop, Investigate, Find, and Trace. It's a media literacy strategy promoted by digital information expert Mike Caulfield (2019) to help students find credible online information. Caulfield leads the University of Washington Information School's Center for an Informed Public, a rapid-response research program that tracks online mis- and disinformation, especially during elections and crisis events. He developed the SIFT approach based on Weinberg's work at SHEG.

Caulfield offers a compelling example of how difficult it is to accurately assess the quality of online information. He describes a 2017 experiment by the SHEG research group (Wineburg & McGrew, 2017) that asked three groups of people—professional historians, Stanford students, and professional fact-checkers—to compare two websites in five minutes to determine which was most credible.

The first website the groups examined was the American Academy of Pediatrics, an organization of 60,000 doctors and scientists and considered one of the most authoritative bodies of experts on the health and well-being of children. The second website was the American College of Pediatricians, founded to protest the adoption of children by same-sex couples, considered by many to be a single-issue hate group.

The results of the survey were shocking:

- 50% of the professional historians chose the non-credible website
- 65% of Stanford students chose the non-credible website
- 100% of the fact-checkers chose the legitimate medical site

How did the fact-checkers get it right, not even using the full five minutes? They employed quick-check strategies, like SIFT, that the professional historians and Stanford students did not think to use.

Teach your students all four steps, and they will be well on their way to being able to accurately assess online information.

S is for Stop

The first step of the SIFT approach happens immediately upon opening a web page. Stop and ask two quick questions:

- Do I know and trust the website or source?
- Is it what I expected before I clicked?

The answers may be *yes* (continue research) or *no* or *maybe* (stop reading and engage the next three SIFT steps). This first step is a metacognitive pause, where students rely on intuition and experience to make a quick judgment. "Stop" gets them to reflexively think about and interpret what they see before spending more time on a website. As they gain more experience with SIFT, this first step goes faster.

"Stop" also helps address a familiar problem with online research: going down information rabbit holes. Students can get caught up in a frenzy of clicking, chasing ever more obscure facts, hopping from one website to the next. This first SIFT strategy also reminds young researchers who find themselves getting farther afield to stop and ask themselves: *What's my goal?* The answer to this simple question can get them back on track by helping recall the purpose of their search, naturally causing them to adjust the search depth and breadth by being more selective with their clicking.

Information rabbit holes can be far worse than a frustrating waste of time for impressionable young people, however. The Southern Poverty Law Center (2018) produced a five-minute video about online radicalization that teachers may wish to consider using with their classes. Titled "The Miseducation of Dylann Roof," it explains how search engine algorithms helped influence a white teenager to murder nine Black churchgoers in Charleston, South Carolina, in 2015.

The video explains how the teen "typed 'Black on white crime' into Google" and was never "the same since that day." Search engine algorithms catering to user preferences in order to hold his attention fed Roof more and more online hate materials. He went down a disinformation rabbit hole, and his online world soon seemed dominated by hate for white people. Submerged in the search results was the truth about Black on white crime: FBI crime statistics prove far more white people are killed by other white people than by Black people.

Ask students to reflect in writing about their own experiences with internet rabbit holes and instances when they've lost track of their search purpose.

I is for Investigate the Source

The second move in the SIFT approach helps students make sense of search results and is used if students click on an article from a source with which they are not familiar. Like the professional fact-checkers in the Stanford study, they can quickly investigate source background by using Wikipedia. Yes, Wikipedia! Once mostly avoided as a student tool by K–12 educators, Wikipedia has become over the last decade a far more reliable research tool in school. It now has stricter rules around sourcing facts, and the nonprofit organization also requires articles to adopt neutral points of view.

One element that hasn't changed about Wikipedia is that the content is curated and edited by volunteer contributors from anywhere in the world and is subject to constant modification. This makes Wikipedia entries inappropriate and unreliable to use as primary sources in scholastic or journalistic writing.

So how do fact-checkers quickly use Wikipedia to help them determine the validity of information online? When they see information from a source they don't know—on a website or via social media—they read no further. Instead, they check out what the crowd-sourced encyclopedia is saying about the source: *Who are these people or this organization?*

Here's the process:

1. Go to Wikipedia.
2. Type in the name of the source—the company, agency, publication, or expert that is sharing the information—to see if they have a Wikipedia entry. (If they don't, it's a potential red flag that requires a broader web search.)

3. Read the Wikipedia entry to determine if they seem credible.
   a. How long have they been around?
   b. What's their budget or revenue source?
   c. Do they have a lot of subscribers or customers?
   d. Any awards from respected organizations?
4. Scroll to the bottom of the Wiki entry to see if linked footnotes lead to reputable publications.

Doing this takes a minute or two, allowing fact-checkers to quickly understand the difference between, for example, Reuters (an international news outlet with 200 locations around the world) and Russia Today, also known as RT (a government propaganda outlet).

It's an easy way to determine whether a so-called expert works for a renowned academic institution, has written for a legitimate publication and received well-known prizes or published well-received books, or is someone with no such references.

To give your students practice, prepare a list of corporations, publications, and famous people and then use Wikipedia to determine if they would be credible sources for a particular issue (e.g., teen vaping, the effects of social media on teens, or how weather affects teen moods). Have students write a brief paragraph about a source's credibility, using evidence from Wikipedia to support their claims.

F is for Find Better Coverage

The third move after "Stop" and "Investigate the Source" is "Find Better Coverage," a technique that helps students dig into claims they might encounter through sources that are not entirely credible. Perhaps the source is dubious, but the claim has a degree of truth? Professional fact-checkers use at least three ways to check it out:

- News aggregators, such as Google News
- Specialty fact-checking websites, such as Snopes
- Reverse-image search

A news aggregator is one of the quickest ways to find better coverage. Google News, for example, pulls breaking news from more than 50,000 online news outlets across the world. A plane crash or celebrity death, if real, will appear almost immediately on Google News, with multiple outlets reporting. The site also categorizes and prominently highlights fact-checked articles by major news organizations that have verified important breaking news or investigated the veracity of claims made by prominent individuals, such as politicians. A note of caution: news aggregators are imperfect. Their algorithms can miss small or local stories or bury them farther down in the search results than most readers will look.

Specialty websites such as Snopes.com and FactCheck.org are important fact-check tools for students to consider using. The websites sort myths and rumors from legitimate news, updating their front pages quickly as popular claims and rumors sweep across the internet. Along with text, provocative viral images are also investigated and analyzed, and each claim or image is labeled true, false, mixed, or unverifiable.

A third tool that students can use is the reverse-image search, which helps assess the credibility of published photographs. Simply right-click an image in Google Chrome and select "Search Google for Image." (For phones, tap the image and you will get the same menu.) The search results will pull up other instances of the photo on the web, allowing students to quickly ascertain if the image has been published in reputable news outlets or, conversely, if it's only found on social media or websites that lack credible sourcing.

This procedure can also help students spot digitally edited or otherwise altered images by comparing them to the original published image. Professional news outlets do not allow selective editing of news photographs (an ethical violation), but surreptitiously edited photos can flourish unchecked on social media. There are also a variety of websites, such as TinEye.com, that will perform reverse image searches, allowing students to cross-reference search results.

Set aside some time in class for students to casually examine the Snopes website by reading the latest articles and noting the verification labels and their definitions. They can cross-check the day's hot topics by entering keywords from Snopes headlines into a news aggregator such as Google News to check how media outlets are responding. (Some are getting quite fast at labeling fake news.) Encourage students to use Snopes photos to do a reverse-image search to see if they are being shared in other places across the internet.

You may be pleasantly surprised by your students' level of engagement for these types of activities, as one high school teacher shared with us recently:

"We did this activity today in class. Best comment of the day: 'Why haven't we learned all this before now? This is so important to know how to check information!' (Yes . . . that was yelled!)."

T is for Trace Back to the Original Context

The final SIFT move is to trace a claim back to its original context. Students may be aware that news travels quickly over the web, but they may not know how it can morph from publication to publication as it gets rewritten and repurposed. Like the childhood game of telephone, facts might start out as well-sourced and credible in one article and by the time they reach the 3rd— or 20th—rewrite, they may be exaggerated, distorted, or misleading.

For example, consider a social media post in which a popular coach says, "Time to ditch the sunscreen!" linked to an article titled "FDA Warns Chemicals from Sunscreen Enter Your Bloodstream After One Day" (Cooper, 2019). Students click the article (which is real and was first posted on the website Moms.com in May 2019). Skimming it, they might notice the phrase "published in JAMA" is hyperlinked. *The Journal of the American Medical Association* is a peer-reviewed medical journal, and this reference adds a great deal of credibility to the article.

However, please teach your students that a link doesn't mean anything on its own. In fact, clicking that link takes us not to the original JAMA research but instead to a CNN.com article titled "Sunscreen Enters Bloodstream After Just One Day of Use" (LaMotte, 2019). Now the coach's claim is starting to sound credible, because CNN is a major, well-known news outlet, but students who take the time to skim the CNN article will discover something very interesting. A legitimate medical expert makes the opposite claim from the coach. As the CNN article states:

> So, should you stop using sunscreen? Absolutely not, experts say.
>
> "Studies need to be performed to evaluate this finding and determine whether there are true medical implications to absorption of certain ingredients," said Yale School of Medicine dermatologist Dr. David Leffell, a spokesman for the American Academy of Dermatology. He added that in the meantime, people should "continue to be aggressive about sun protection."

The above quote from Leffell didn't make it to the Moms.com article, not even paraphrased. Yet that is critical information that directly affects anyone trying to decide whether to ditch their sunscreen.

You can use the above example in the classroom with students by presenting them with the hypothetical coach scenario and then showing them the real Moms.com digital article. Simply ask them to determine the answer to one question: *Is it responsible for you to "share" or "like" the coach's post?*

Students can use Wikipedia to check the reputations of the Moms.com website, of CNN, and of the named sources, including Dr. David Leffell, whose Wikipedia entry shows his medical education and professional background. In just a few minutes, students should be able to determine that sharing or liking the hypothetical coach's advice is not responsible and could even cause harm.

Once your students are comfortable with the four SIFT moves, it's a good time to have them use the process to check the credibility of the articles they've been using for their initial research on their issue of choice. *Are the experts and news outlets you've gathered credible? Should any be scratched?* With these four strategies in their tool kit, they will be much better prepared to decide what is news and what is not.

Examining Degrees of Bias: How Do We Know What's True?

Before moving into more research or moving on to other stages of the project, we need to help students navigate one more valley in the information landscape: news bias. In a world that is overheated with claims of misinformation, disinformation, and bias, teachers are understandably concerned with how to teach informative reading and writing or even how to talk about current events.

A high school English teacher notes his reservations about teaching with informative texts:

> I'm worried that my students will think that any dialogue I lead about the news will be biased. When I teach fiction, I can talk about big ideas in our world that a story calls attention to. I will not lie, there is a safety when I hide behind a story. I'm sure this anxiety will erode as I get skill in navigating informational texts for a classroom experience, as opposed to personal enrichment.

Direct instruction about bias is essential because it's a term that's used quite casually—and often wrongly—in online communication. Briefly remind students about the difference between news, opinion, and advertising from previous lessons. They should recall that opinion writing is clearly and purposefully biased, as is advertising, while news writing strives to be free from bias.

Next, introduce students to these terms:

- *Bias:* when a writer conveys a particular feeling or attitude, accidentally or on purpose, through a selection of facts, choice of words, and quality and tone of description
- *Story angle:* the article's main point, theme, frame, or lens through which the writer filters and focuses gathered information to make it meaningful to viewers or readers
- *Hyperbole:* extreme exaggeration used to amplify a point

Naturally, everyone has personal biases. Humans are opinionated by nature, as anyone who's spent time around a toddler can attest. It turns out that we're much more likely to see biases in others than in ourselves (Pronin et al., 2002). Understanding what biases are is the first step to identifying them in ourselves, others, and the media we use.

An easy-to-grasp example of bias is when people hold certain opinions about political candidates—not based on what they stand for—but on their name, gender, age, attractiveness, race, educational background, job, or where they live. We tend to think that people we share traits with will think like we do or will have the same values. You can help students consider bias in a more nuanced way by teaching two terms:

- *Implicit bias:* unconscious biases that writers have that they don't recognize, often based on their culture or upbringing
- *Explicit bias:* conscious biases or prejudices that writers know they have

Students can think about how biases occur beyond individual people and show up in our institutions, like journalism. After all, institutions are made of and by people, so they can't escape bias. In fact, biases may be baked into the very structure of how an organization or an institution works. For example, media outlets are subject to economic pressures. This means that who owns a media outlet and who advertises in it can influence or shape the kind of news that is covered and produced.

Media outlets are also subject to political biases: which stories get (and don't get) coverage, how much space a story receives, what kind of framing is used for a story, who the sources are, and whose interests the story represents are all places where an institution's political biases may be evident.

Journalists who report the news cannot escape biases either. They have them. Their sources have them. Their readers have them. Journalists do attempt to recognize and set aside personal beliefs and opinions while reporting. They try to conduct research in a way that allows the most full and accurate story to be told so readers can make up their own minds.

Student journalistic writers should be taught to:

- try to recognize their own preferences and beliefs and to choose a topic that they feel they can research while setting aside personal opinions
- seek out a range of sources to interview to present information from different angles
- present a source's opinion only if it's backed up by facts
- avoid hyperbole
- avoid tone words

In the list above, perhaps the most difficult literary concept for students of any age is identifying an author's tone, as many language arts teachers will attest. Students often know they feel something from reading a text, but they tend to have trouble identifying and explaining how and exactly where their feelings arise. Tone indicates the writer's attitude, and words in a text often convey the author's feelings about a topic with various degrees of subtlety. Perhaps the author is sympathetic, angry, cynical, or hopeful. But professional styles of news writing minimize the author's tone and cloaks the reporter's feelings.

One activity that can help with tone is to ask your students to analyze two short texts about the same topic in order to compare the tones. Just know that it's nearly impossible to find published examples from well-regarded news outlets because any hints of the journalist's attitude are typically cut in editing. It might be necessary to use two entertainment articles, since they are allowed a greater degree of tone and attitude.

For example, students might compare the following two article excerpts about a video game release:

Bad News: "Mario Kart Tour" On Mobile Has Nasty Microtransactions
    . . . There are a lot of strategies for monetization out there that don't feel as oppressive as these, and that's why it's disappointing to see Nintendo go down this road.

We'll see how things develop: maybe we'll be pleasantly surprised when this thing leaves beta. I'm a little pessimistic, however. —*Forbes* (Thier, 2019)

"Mario Kart Tour" Beta Locks Powerful "Rare" Characters Behind Paywall
   . . . As for the game itself, beyond monetization, from initial impressions of screenshots and the like being shared around, it looks like classic "Mario Kart" in portrait mode, with gameplay a bit more simplified. The racer reportedly just drives automatically, and players have to steer by pulling to the left or right. —*Variety* (Lanier, 2019)

Ask students to identify words in the above excerpts that show the writers' attitudes. In the *Forbes* article, they should note the use of: "oppressive," "disappointing" and "pessimistic" to show the writer's negative attitude about the game. The *Variety* article, however, lacks a tone and focuses on facts, hiding the author's attitude about the game, showing less bias.

One simple way for students to avoid adding unintentional tone to their informative writing is to have them identify adjectives or adverbs in their descriptions.

For example, if they write:

"The food bank manager works incredibly hard to make sure there are enough fresh vegetables," you can help students notice the adjective–adverb pairing "incredibly hard" and explain how it creates a sympathetic opinion of the manager.

Delete the words to create a less apparent authorial voice:

"The food bank manager makes sure there are enough fresh fruits and vegetables."

Decisions about sources should also be examined for bias:

- How many sources were questioned?
- How many quotes were given to each source?
- How are the sources positioned in the article (first, last, etc.)?

In an ideal world of unlimited time, money, and access, journalists would present detailed information from all angles, interviewing and quoting many sources. In the real world of news reporting, however, there is typically the need to balance time and resources. For reporters, it often becomes a serious ethical dilemma: *Considering my limitations, how do I equitably, accurately, and fairly cover this issue or event?*

Students should know that reporting often gets to a "good enough" stage. Maybe it's not good enough for all readers, but this is why specialty publications thrive alongside general news outlets, providing more in-depth coverage. It's also why guest opinions and letters to the editor have a place in the daily newspaper. And it's why the biggest, best funded news outlets can publish the most in-depth reporting, while local news often suffers from surface reporting due to fewer resources.

Teaching with a Unit-Long Mentor Text

Students learning about bias really need to dig into a carefully selected news article to do some of the above-mentioned analysis. Introducing a mentor text they can use for the remainder of the project is an excellent idea at this stage. A single multifaceted article can help illuminate all phases of journalistic learning. Returning again and again to a single article can lower some of the cognitive strain felt by some students (including English learners or students with differing reading abilities), allowing them to focus more on the new reading and writing skills being introduced.

One article we recommend is "Starlings in Oregon are an Invasive Pest to Some, a Fascinating Species Facing 'Bio Bigotry' to Others" by Megan Banta (2021) of *The Register-Guard* in Eugene, Oregon. (See Appendix B for the full article.)

This well-researched article provides an opportunity for students to examine bias by looking at

- evidence of the author's voice. *Are there tone words?*
- number and types of sources. *Is the issue presented from different angles?*
- source equity. *Who gets more quotes? Who is positioned first and last?*
- representation. *Who is privileged? How are the voiceless represented?*

You might ask students to work in pairs to identify direct and paraphrased statements from sources, sorting them into two sides of the issue: the positives and negatives of starlings. Next, have students highlight words the author used that might convey tone and circle any examples of hyperbole. Students can then discuss or write answers to the following four questions:

1. Is the headline balanced, or does it lean pro- or anti-starling?
2. Is a positive or negative tone conveyed in the unquoted information?
3. Does the reporter allow one source or side to dominate the article?

4. Since the starlings can't speak for themselves, do they get fair representation? Could the reporter have done more?

Ask students to mark a spot on a bias line (as shown below) and write a justification for their decision.

More Biased --**X----** **Less Biased**

Finally, the class can compare their decisions and discuss their reasoning and evidence.

Just as there is no one theme to a poem or literary short story, there is no single right or wrong answer to the question: *Is this article biased?* It's always a matter of degree. However, we believe Banta's article about the starlings can be placed closer to the Less Biased side of the line. This is due to its neutral tone, the lack of hyperbole, and the balance of sources. The sheer number of sources for a local article of this length is impressive, with multiple people quoted from the academic, regulatory, and service sectors, stating in their own words what they know and believe to be true about the issue and the species.

If your students are having difficulty deciding the degree of bias in the article, ask them to imagine the reporter had never interviewed some of the sources (or didn't include their views in the article). For example, if quotes from the ornithology professor or the bird store owner were deleted, it's easy to see how the article loses its balance.

You may find that some students are especially attuned to viewing the article from the starlings' perspective. Students might assert, for example, that the article shows a greater degree of bias in favor of humans over birds, noting the number of words devoted to informing readers how to deter and eliminate starlings versus how to assist and protect them. This is certainly arguable, and arguments of this type are to be encouraged. The class does not need to agree; we encourage teachers to allow students to form their own opinions. These types of arguments take a great deal of critical thinking and ask students to draw on moral reasoning. The arguments also present a high level of engagement and help new concepts stick.

Whatever mentor text is chosen, it's best if it is printed out for students to mark up by hand and save for reference. The handout will be useful to return to throughout the research, inquiry, interviewing, writing, and editing stages of the project. We will be providing examples in later chapters of how to do this using the "Starlings" article (and you can see the full text in Appendix B).

How to Approach the Problem of Biased Media Outlets

Teachers may worry about offending students—and families of students—who believe the news they read or watch is unbiased, when in fact it doesn't meet a standard of neutral reporting. One middle school teacher explained:

> I think, for me, one concern I have regarding flexibility and a journalism curriculum is answering questions on facts. For example, I dread the day that a student asks me if a certain highly politicized "news" outlet is a reliable source. I value honesty in my communication—both as a professional and a person. I would hate to be put in a position where giving an honest answer to a question erodes trust between myself and my community of students. I am sure I will manage to navigate that, however. I will continue to hold my students in a positive regard, and that will carry me through the difficult conversations.

Instructors can approach this problem by giving students the chance to analyze how major media outlets treat a breaking news story. Choose a contemporary event with political ramifications, for example the announcement of a new Supreme Court justice nominee. Find four articles on the topic from four different major media outlets. A good selection would be articles from the BBC (to offer an international perspective), MSNBC (which skews to the political left), Fox News (which skews to the political right), and the Associated Press (which runs in local news outlets across the country).

Have students highlight words that convey tone and compare them across the four articles. Then ask students to discuss:

- What overall tone is created in each of the articles (e.g., negative, positive, pessimistic, optimistic, etc.)?
- Which words create the tones?

Ask students to examine the types of sources that are quoted and paraphrased:

- How many sources appear in each article?
- Who or what do the sources speak for (e.g., organization, geographical area, past, present)?

- Who speaks first and last? (These are positions in the article that convey more importance.)
- How many times does each source get quoted? (Is there a balance?)
- How does the international article compare to the domestic articles?
- How does the Associated Press article compare to the MSNBC and Fox articles?

Finally, ask them to place all four articles on the bias line and explain their reasoning. Discuss in table groups or as a class: *Which article shows the least bias, and how can you tell?*

Biased --- **Less Biased**

Giving middle and high school students the analytical techniques to examine bias in any news article they run across takes the burden off teachers to serve as arbiters of reliability. It's far more meaningful and less controversial than banning outlets from the classroom.

So now the stage is set. With the tools to efficiently evaluate information for credibility and bias in hand, students should be able to move with confidence into the next part of the project: crafting great questions and connecting with community experts.

Journalistic Skills for Every Career: Human Resources

People who work in human resources need to set aside judgment about employees in order to help resolve conflicts. Their job is to listen carefully to all sides of an issue at work and help employees work out problems. They are expected to be impartial, not show favorites, listen to evidence, and become aware of their own implicit biases.

CHAPTER 5

Crafting Great Questions

"Interviewing professionals in the community takes students out of their bubble. It's an important step in growing to be a more proactive citizen, instead of just allowing things to happen."

—11th-Grade History and English Teacher

ASKING QUESTIONS AND GETTING ANSWERS. Requesting help and receiving it. Such a simple concept, and so powerful for human development and relations. Yet technology makes it ever easier to circumvent person-to-person contact. We save time by getting immediate online assistance from digital chatbots, those interactive computer programs that hold human-like conversations with us online. We compare dozens of potential solutions to a problem by crowd-sourcing our questions on social media. No question is too obscure for the web.

What may be slipping away, especially among our youth, is the experience of connecting with people in real life, in the here and now. Many would rather turn to their screens for help than to the nearest actual person.

Journalistic learning builds social capacity in young people by embedding essential real-time inquiry into their work. When they talk to adults about issues they wonder about, students' sense of social connection to a community grows alongside their confidence. They feel more agency as they interview people who are working on problems in their own town, potentially on behalf of their friends, neighbors, and family. They become insiders for a little while, gaining special knowledge that they can interpret and share with others.

Unlike a video, conversation is alive. It's an experience. Interviews have energy and intensity, with a sense of give and take and of possibility and surprise. Interviews are not just boring transfers of information; they can be dynamic exchanges of concern.

This is all the more important because America has a growing trust problem. Younger Americans, far more than other age groups, say they distrust institutions and other people. A 2019 Pew study reported that a whopping 60% of 18- to 29-year-olds think "most people can't be trusted," compared to just 29% of the 65-plus age group (Gramlich, 2019). Hot takes, contrary views, and unsolicited advice are everywhere now, and social media is damaging the traditional routes of how we identify expertise.

Today, it seems that no matter how extreme an opinion or claim is, there's someone online to back it up. Actual experts, competing in a glut of content, find it hard to distinguish themselves. The COVID-19 pandemic is a case study. Millions of Americans turned away from the advice of highly trained and experienced epidemiologists and public health professionals in order to follow much less reputable online and offline self-declared experts touting unproven theories and sketchy medical treatments via slick digital video production, memes, and posts. Teaching young people to connect with proven sources of good local information is imperative.

While the previous chapter emphasized reading texts critically and sifting through the noise of misinformation, this chapter details how you can help students find information firsthand. Who can they talk to from their community? What will they ask? How can they frame their questions and organize their research? What kinds of facts do they need to gather in order to write accurate and engaging stories? We'll walk you through how to lead your students to develop their inquiry and outreach techniques and invite local experts into the classroom.

Finding Sources: Rule Makers, Researchers, and Helpers

Before they develop specific questions around their topic, help your students step back from the particulars of their chosen issue to consider three broad sources of local information: the regulatory, academic, and service sectors. Each may offer a unique perspective about the ways a complex issue manifests in your community. We've nicknamed these categories of sources the rule makers, the researchers, and the helpers.

Rule Makers

Who makes and oversees the rules around this issue? The regulatory sector includes local government experts as well as state and federal government employees working at the community level. These are people who make and uphold the laws. They might include elected officials, such as a city council member, a school board member, a county supervisor, or a state senator. They might also include unelected government employees who work in regulatory affairs.

Researchers

Who researches and teaches about this issue? Professors and subject experts at local universities and colleges, particularly those engaged with research around the issue and how it impacts the community, can be great resources. These people also tend to be excited and willing to talk about their areas of expertise. Students also might find valuable, practical information closer to home by looking for academic sources in their own school district, such as a principal, district director, or superintendent.

Helpers

Who aids those affected by this issue? The service sector can be subdivided into at least three subcategories:

- government employees who provide public services
- nonprofit or religious organization employees who help serve the larger community
- private businesspeople who sell goods or services

It's useful at this stage of the journalistic project to show students a well-sourced news article and have them identify the sources the reporter used. Ask your students to sort the sources into the above categories so they can notice the range of people the journalist spoke to. Are there any who don't fit into the categories? Are there nonexperts who were interviewed, such as customers, clients, patients, victims, or passersby?

Using our mentor text "Starlings in Oregon," for example, students would note six different sources that the journalist Megan Banta included:

Regulatory (Rule makers):
1. Rick Boatner, Invasive Species Coordinator, Oregon Department of Fish & Wildlife

Academic (Researchers):
2. Jenifer Cruikshank, assistant professor, Oregon State University
3. Dan Gleason, former professor of ornithology, University of Oregon

Service (Helpers):

4. Barbara and Dan Gleason, owners of Wild Birds Unlimited (local business)
5. Devon Ashbridge, spokeswoman, Short Mountain Landfill (county government)
6. Angie Marzano, specialist with Lane County Waste Management (county government)

Each of these sources adds a distinct perspective to the problem of starlings in the community. The constituents they represent—farmers, birdwatchers, waste workers, scientists—see this invasive species differently. If starlings could talk, they'd have something to add, too.

Of course, due to time and inexperience, your students will not be interviewing six sources for their project. We recommend they identify two potential sources from each category—six total. They will only interview one of them live and try to ask questions of two more by email. Of course, if they want to contact all six, they can certainly go for it.

Searching for Local Experts

The quest for local sources starts online. Students will likely need guidance on how to do productive searches for local experts because conducting an online search of the first questions that come to mind is probably not going to work. It may be helpful to teach students to move from a general question, *Who can I talk to about birds?* or *Who's an expert on birds?* to a more specific string of search terms.

First, show them how to change general words to more specific ones.

bird → starlings
expert → ornithologist
local → "Eugene, Oregon"

In this example, a general search, *local bird expert,* becomes a specific one: *starlings ornithologist Eugene Oregon.*

If they are unaware, teach students to use lists of specific nouns, separated by commas, and to place related words in quotes:

- Landfill, starlings, "Lane County, Oregon"
- "Wild birds," business, "Eugene, Oregon"

- "Wild bird," pests, laws, Oregon
- "Wild birds," "Lane County," "tips to prevent"
- Starlings, complaints, "Eugene, Oregon"
- Starlings, university, Oregon, ornithology

Notice how some of the above queries are specific to the city, while others name the county or just the state. Some include "starlings," others use "wild birds." Students should be taught to adjust their queries to be more or less specific until they hit a sweet spot. Too narrow and they may miss great sources working just outside their community. Too wide and they could overlook sources close to home.

Developing Their North Star Question

Before students finalize their source list or contact any experts, they should achieve a degree of clarity about what they hope to find out. This doesn't mean generating every question now—there are specific strategies to use in this area, as we'll explain in a bit. What they need at this stage is to create a single overarching question that will serve to frame their inquiry.

An overarching question, one that is neither too small nor too large, is what we call the North Star of a journalistic research project—the orienting constant, as it were. Teachers might think of this as the essential questions that are often posed at the start of a course unit. English language arts teachers who have helped students learn to discover themes in literary texts will notice the similarity. Themes in poems and stories can bring cohesiveness and reveal an author's deeper message. Overarching questions in journalistic learning can help young writers streamline their inquiry and organize their information. Finding their North Star question now also helps students succinctly communicate the purpose of their research when they connect with local experts.

A quick analysis activity is a good way to help students understand this concept. Using your mentor text, prepare a list of questions for them to consider, ranging from narrow to broad in scope and engaging all of the 5 Ws and H questions: who, what, where, when, why, and how. Then have them discuss and sort the questions. For example, from the "Starlings" article, students could imagine the reporter might have wondered the following:

What crops do starlings eat? (narrow)
Where do starlings nest? (narrow)

Do farmers like starlings? (narrow)

Do bird-watchers like starlings? (narrow)

When did starlings first arrive in Eugene? (narrow)

How do starlings impact local agriculture? (narrow)

Why are starlings a pest in Eugene? (broad)

Do the positives of starlings in Eugene outweigh the negatives? (broad)

Either of the last two questions could have served as Banta's North Star, guiding her research and interviews, helping her quickly communicate with potential sources the angle of her story. Either question also would help her not waste time following a trail of unnecessary trivia about starlings.

After this type of activity, you can ask students to review the questions they've prepared so far for their own issue. They should select (or if necessary, create) one of them to be their North Star question. You might have them present it to the class for feedback, and suggest they keep revising it until they have a question that strikes the right balance.

Introducing a Narrative Structure for Student Inquiry

We're not big believers in giving students templates for major writing assignments because such templates often oversimplify the messy, deep, complicated work of thinking and drafting, leaving young people ill-prepared to write independently. However, we have found a loose organizing structure can be quite helpful for beginning writers, and we have successfully used a journalistic narrative frame for both the inquiry and writing phases of the project. This frame has students develop questions in three broad categories:

1. *The Present:* How are things now?
2. *The Past:* How did things get this way?
3. *The Future:* What might happen next?

It helps here if your mentor text is organized using this structure. For example, in the "Starlings" text, students can identify exactly where Banta transitioned from present-day facts and opinions about starlings to historical information about the species, before shifting back to the present again. She saved future-oriented information, along with advice or potential solutions, for the last third of the article.

Present. Past. Future.

It's a storytelling frame that works. It's likely that Banta's questions were organized this way, too. Noticing this type of framing in a news article is often a great relief for students, who may be either a bit overwhelmed at the breadth and depth of journalistic inquiry or somewhat overly reliant on the standard five-paragraph essay structure.

To help students begin to dig deeper into their own budding inquiry, a nice activity is to ask them to try to reverse engineer the mentor text to imagine the actual questions a reporter might have asked. Have them read a small section of text and write in the margins the questions that could have elicited each fact and opinion from a source. For example, from the "Starlings" article, students could read this section:

> They also do damage on grass fields, Boatner said.
> Starlings have a long beak and can pull up and eat planted seeds, hindering crop production.
> They generally don't enjoy seeds, Dan Gleason said, but they do like to eat apples, blueberries, cherries, strawberries, figs and many other cultivated fruits.

From here, they might surmise the reporter asked sources:

> *What damage do starlings do?*
> *In what ways do starlings hurt agriculture in our area?*
> *What crops are most affected by starlings?*

Younger students might offer that the journalist asked, *What do starlings eat?* However, this is an example of an unrefined, overly general question that would probably lead to irrelevant information. If your students produce these types of questions, remind them to keep the purpose of their writing at the forefront of all they do. The goal is not to write a Wikipedia-type article. It's to share a story about a community issue, providing readers only the information that helps inform them about the issue. The exercise described above can help students shift their perspective from readers and researchers to writers. It also prepares them to develop more granular questions for their interviews.

Now is a good time to have your students go back to their own growing list of questions and start to categorize them into the present-past-future frame. They can make a simple three-column chart or use three separate pieces of paper and place their questions into the categories. They may realize they have gaping holes. Maybe all of their questions are concerned with the present and they need to focus on the past and future. There is still plenty of time to develop questions, and we'll give examples of how to do so with more activities in the upcoming sections.

Prepping the Final Source List

Your students at this point will naturally be looking around online for more local sources. Encourage and provide time for the circularity of journalistic inquiry, allowing them to glide back and forth from opaque and vague wondering to more concrete question development. You might want to set a soft deadline for them to match their initial questions to the experts they hope to contact.

Eventually, reporting teams should come up with a specific wish list of local sources they would like to question, either in person, in a video chat, or via email. Encourage students to aim big. Even busy, important adults often are willing to help students understand local challenges in more detail. It never hurts to ask.

Reviewing students' source lists allows you to note if they are grasping the breadth and depth of their chosen issue and if they are localizing their inquiry. You also might have students reflect in writing about which source they most want to interview live in front of the class. *Which one might be the most interesting to other students? Which potentially has the most specific information they can use? Who are their first and second choices?* This type of reflection can help students home in on the source they prefer to interview live, as well as allow them to visualize their future interview. It can also give you a sense of student engagement, motivation, and progress. (See Table A.2 in Appendix A for an example of a source organizer you can adapt for students to organize contact information.)

The power of live interviews cannot be exaggerated. They are what distinguish this project from traditional academic papers. Making contact and getting commitments, however, takes strategy, patience, and sometimes persistence for students. It all starts with email.

Writing Professional Emails

What can we say about student emails? They're sometimes humorous, sometimes unintentionally rude, sometimes difficult to take seriously, and sometimes nearly impossible to understand. If you have ever gotten an email from a student with the entire text placed in the subject line instead of the body, you know what we're talking about. Direct instruction on how to write a professional quality email is probably a necessity since it's one of those writing practices we always assume has been covered in earlier grades.

Your students may be surprised to learn that many adults are pleased to talk to them about their work, even flattered that someone has noticed it. Some will bend over backwards to assist a student with genuine questions. However, this can never be assumed. In our era of email scams and online hoaxes, many adults are wary of emails from strangers. If there are doubts about the legitimacy of the request, potential sources may ignore a well-meaning student inquiry. Unlike teachers, they have little motivation to labor over a student email that is filled with grammatical or spelling errors, is confusing, or that reads as if it could be a prank.

Email requests to sources should follow professional norms in order to have the best chance of being answered. Students should take seriously the fact that an email is a first impression and is more formal than texting or messaging on social media. You might wish to start off a conversation about email effectiveness by presenting two contrasting examples, as illustrated in Figure 5.1.

The difference between the two examples is more than obvious, but exaggeration can help students quickly see potential communication barriers. Some students seem to have a more difficult time shifting perspectives from themselves as a writer who (they think) is clearly making an appeal to a reader who is trying to decipher a novel request from a stranger. Ask students: *What are the aspects of these emails that make them more or less likely to be answered?* Have them notice the varying degrees of formality of the language, spelling, clarity, and effort.

Reporting teams should choose just one source to ask for a live interview, either in person in the classroom or over a video chat that is broadcast live to the class. But they should also create a Plan B and even C, because there's a chance their first choice will cancel. This raises the issue of how one best handles not offending their backup persons. Students can generally write, "I'm researching a story about _____. I'm not yet sure who will be the key/central

FIGURE 5.1 **Examples of appropriate and inappropriate emails to sources can help students preview and avoid potential communication barriers.**

First Impressions Matter

Imagine you get two emails requesting help. What do you notice?

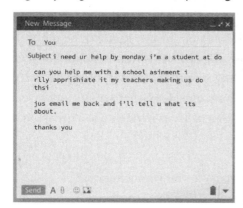
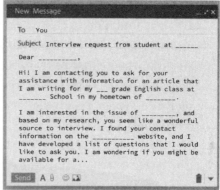

Credit: The Journalistic Learning Initiative

source for my story. Are you available around _____ (date), should I decide to interview you?" Honesty is the best policy, should they need to make a short-notice request of one of their backups.

Professional emails follow certain norms, and this is the one time in the project that we believe a formal writing template is productive since it's the style of the writing that is complex, not the content. Business emails are short, courteous, and clear, with succinct subject headers and a well-organized body. In this project, they should include:

1. A salutation (with correct spelling of person's name)
2. An introduction of who they are
   - Names
   - Grade
   - School
   - Teacher
3. An explanation of the project
   - The goal
   - The overarching question
   - A couple sample questions (with answers that can't easily be found online)

4. A timeline for response
   - Window of time for interviews to take place
   - When an answer is needed (with at least a week to respond to the email)
5. A polite closing

You may find it necessary to instill some guardrails that will help limit misunderstandings or conflicts. To prevent students from accidentally sending an unfinished email or from sending one that is not quite up to par, consider having them draft email requests outside of their email software first, such as on paper or in a digital document. Peer reviews are a great idea and can include:

- What questions does the email make you wonder about?
- Are there grammar or spelling mistakes?
- Did all required information get included?
- As a busy professional, how likely would you be to answer this email? Why?

You also might wish to review and approve email drafts in advance, since they reflect the project and your instruction. You can require that students copy you on any emails they send. Or they can add your email or phone number to the body of text so the recipient knows how to contact you directly with any questions. Some middle school teachers prefer to remain the point of contact by sending emails to prospective sources on behalf of students.

If a source declines an interview request, students should move to their

TABLE 5.1 Sample Class Interview Sign-up Sheet

Date	Day	Period 2 Time	Appt.	Name of Source	Occupation or Company	Reporting Team
1/10	Mon.	9:03 – 10:00	9:15	Robert C. Source	The Source Factory	Xochitl, Travis, Emily
1/11	Tues.	9:03 – 10:00				
1/12	Wed.	9:03 – 10:00				

second choice and on down the list until someone commits. Once a source is lined up, students can reserve other sources for email-only interviews or for phone calls or brief video chats, if they are ambitious. A class sign-up sheet like the sample in Table 5.1 is helpful so students do not double book in-class interviews.

Overcoming Interview Barriers

Scheduling class interviews is perhaps the most challenging stage of the journalistic learning project, because it is outside students' control and there are usually unforgiving constraints around class time. Students may have difficulty getting sources to agree to be interviewed or may have trouble getting those who agree to commit to a day and time.

Here are some ideas that may help you and your students overcome barriers:

- *Expand their source lists:* Students may need to keep expanding who they can talk to. Try local experts, then locals who are involved with the issue but might not be experts, then people from out of the area who are experts. If students have just been looking in town, maybe it's time to look in the rest of the state. If they've just been looking in the state, maybe it's time to look at neighboring states.
- *Tap your professional and personal networks:* Depending on the size of your community, the age of your students, or the type of issue they are researching, some students may require offline support. You might have good luck turning to your personal or professional networks. Social media and school emails can be a big help here: *Does anyone in (community) know a local (job type) who can answer my students' questions about (topic)?* Some of the best interviews we've seen with our students were last-minute fills-ins by the principal, other teachers, advisers, and so on. They may not have been experts in the issue at hand, but they had interesting stories and opinions about it, and there was value in students getting to see a different side of educators.
- *Extend the interview window:* If your interview window has come and gone and some students were not able to connect with sources yet, feel free to move on with the project's other components. Give students who aren't having luck a bit more time to conduct their interviews.

- *Allow sources to see questions in advance:* Some sources may request to see student questions in advance of committing to an interview. While traditionally this is not acceptable in journalism, it's a lot to ask an outsider to commit to a live classroom interview. It might be necessary to compromise and provide sources with some information about what students are wondering about. Students could send a few sample questions they know they will ask, while letting the prospective interviewee know there may be other questions, as well. The other approach is not to send specific questions but to say, "I can send you an overview of the areas I plan to discuss. However, we're taught that interviews are most authentic when they are freeform and impromptu."

- *Communicate with sources yourself:* Another consideration is that sources may be worried about "gotcha" journalism (in which a reporter tries to entrap an interviewee into damaging or discrediting their cause, character, integrity, or reputation). They may be concerned that students will ask something embarrassing to which they don't know how to respond. It might be necessary for you to step in to help reassure sources that this is not going to be the case— that questions will be vetted in advance so that they are appropriate to ask in front of the class and that the interview will resemble a respectful student-led class discussion, not a grilling.

Journalistic Skills for Every Career: Real Estate Agent

Real estate agents are always trying to identify and land prospective clients. This means writing a lot of outreach emails. Making a good impression and standing out from their competitors is a must for real estate agents. Over email, they try to achieve the right balance of courtesy and assertiveness—*Yes, I can meet all your needs and here's what we'll do.* A well-written email can leave potential clients with the impression that the agent is competent and that they will be in good hands. It's a critical communication skill that can be the difference between landing a future client or having them slip away to someone else.

Managing the Squishy Middle

By now, your students have crafted their North Star question, are working on a growing list of sub questions, and have identified specific people they want to interview. They've reached out by email to potential sources and are waiting for responses and, hopefully, commitments. Now is the time to help them directly acknowledge the gap that every journalist faces at some point while producing a feature-length article. We call this stage of the project the "squishy middle," and it is not a very comfortable place for students who prefer to stand on solid ground and know exactly where to go and what to do next.

This is the stage where students suddenly notice the holes. They start to see the gulf that exists between what they know and what they should know in order to conduct a live interview or write about their issue. Students may notice that the questions they've drafted so far are vague. They may feel they still don't know what to ask or what facts they should try to find. They probably sense that they understand a lot less than they first thought when they chose the issue of concern. They may even wonder why the heck they chose this topic in the first place. A high school English teacher described it like this:

> I did see a drop in confidence from research fatigue, but as I brought them into the [active inquiry process] and explained the connection between developing new questions and interviewing real sources—the purpose of it—they got reinvigorated.

Fatigue and slipping confidence are normal. For many reporting teams, this stage is a gut check, and they get busy. Other teams may be in denial and feel rising anxiety. Almost all students could use structured help in coming up with great questions, and this is a good time to step away from the mentor text just for a class period or two and have them interact with an unfamiliar news article to look at the types and quantity of details conveyed in ordinary journalistic writing. This likely will help them think of new questions.

You might choose a current event or a high-interest feature story from your local paper. Even the simplest articles are replete with facts that answer the 5 W's and H questions. Once you find a new article, ask students to examine the "lede." In journalistic writing, the beginning of an article is called the lede, which is pronounced "leed" but spelled this way to distinguish it from "lead," the metal that was once used for printing before a press run. As they read, direct students to circle facts that answer *who, what, where, when, why,* and *how.*

Next, guide students to ask themselves, *What are the facts we have gathered about our issue so far?* They can look at their questions, which have been categorized into their past, present, and future frame, and organize any notes that they have taken from their online research. Some of their previous research and questions may seem irrelevant now. Throw them out. Some new questions may pop up. Add them. Students now may be able to connect specific questions to specific sources. *This would be a good person to ask about . . .* Keep building the source list.

Some students—especially younger ones—may feel a bit reluctant to throw out some of their first questions and research. *I already did the work, but now it doesn't matter, so have I failed?* Coach them through any dismaying feelings. Acknowledging that some early questions or notes are now extraneous or uninteresting is not wrong. It's just part of the process. It's like taking a ton of photos or videos but only posting the best ones to Instagram or TikTok. Discovering what's essential is an editing process, and it's a necessary part of any creative inquiry—the convergent flip side of divergent brainstorming.

Other students may suddenly feel a lot less confident at this stage due to a lack of structure. Empathize with them by explaining that writers, scientists, researchers, artists, and people who work to understand or create novel ideas often feel the immensity of an unstructured project exactly here, during the squishy middle, and may also become overwhelmed. Reassure them that some of the gap of what they don't know may be filled by their sources in the coming days and some may be bridged by doing more research online using credible sources.

This part of the project—where students step into the unknown to find their way across—is essential and valuable. It gives them practice with life outside of school. Many tasks placed in front of them post–high school will not be laid out as neatly as they are in the classroom. Directions may not be clear or exist at all. They may need to be self-starters or step into impromptu leadership roles, whether it's at work or to accomplish personal goals. Students who get to work in a classroom environment where the answers are not concrete or automatically forthcoming experience what we now refer to as beneficial stress, the type of frustration that builds stamina and confidence over time.

The squishy middle makes instructors anxious, as well. An 11th-grade teacher describes it as a "nebulous" period:

"This is my first time doing this project, and so I was like 'all right, is this what we're supposed to be doing? Is this the way it's supposed to be happening?' I was trying to reassure myself."

Teachers want their students to be successful and feel confident, and it's hard to watch them flail or listen to them complain. Try to find the right balance with each reporting team, if you can. Support them but insist they take charge of their learning, even if they are nervous or a bit overwhelmed. It is amazing what students are capable of when left to figure it out on their own.

You might want to ask students to individually reflect in writing at this stage of the project: *How do you feel about what you know (or don't know) so far? To what degree is your reporting team on track or lost in the weeds?* This is a good report to collect so that you can informally assess each student's confidence level and discover any budding problems with collaboration or cooperation. Some teams may need refocusing or outright assistance finding sources or background information. For most students, developing new and highly targeted questions is the next logical step.

Getting through the squishy middle is challenging but worth it. As students hone their questions and start to connect with sources, some teachers notice the classroom mood changes. As her students emerged from the squishy and nebulous stage of learning, one 11th-grade teacher was pleased:

> Watching the students light up, because of the choice and their ability to own this project, brings a higher energy to the room that I didn't notice last year when I taught a typical research paper with my 11th-graders. They're truly engaged and enthusiastic to see where it goes. And they're also a little bit shocked when I said, "Oh, we're publishing these. These will be out for the public. It's not just one and done." They are excited.

Using Numbers and Statistics

Numbers help a story resonate. They can allow us to see past assumptions and get specific information. They help us gain clarity, moving us from vague impressions to concrete understanding. Journalistic inquiry leads students to infuse numbers and statistics into their writing so that they examine and present issues with complexity and specificity.

It helps when asking students to work with numbers and statistics to approach these as a reader first, writer second. Working with whatever mentor text you've chosen, ask students to circle or highlight quantitative details in the text:

- Quantities of people
- Ages
- Lengths of time or distance

- Frequency
- Costs or values

They can do the same with statistics, which are used journalistically to describe large quantities and infer proportional relationships. Students can examine the text to see if the journalist uses numbers to describe the scale of a problem, the percentages (comparing parts to a whole), and the rates of change over time.

After students find examples in their mentor text, they should review their own questions, noticing if they've included quantitative or statistical ones. If not, this is the time to add them. Some quantitative question starters are listed in Table 5.2.

TABLE 5.2   Quantitative Question Starters

Ask a source	To get this information
How many _____ are there?	number in group
How old is _____?	age
How long is _____?	length of time or distance
How often does _____?	frequency
How much does _____ cost?	money
How big a problem is _____?	scale
How fast is _____ changing?	rate of change over time
How does _____ compare to _____?	variation
What percentage of _____ is that?	proportion to whole

The goal should be for reporting teams to develop quantitative and statistical questions for all three sections of their narrative frame (present, past, future). Quantifiable facts are sometimes found most easily online, in reports or other news articles, so give students time to search again. They are also more easily asked in written email requests so that sources can take time to track down accurate information.

Gathering Vivid Qualitative Details

Qualitative details add color and bring bare-bones, factual sentences to life. Every English teacher strives to teach students to write vividly in order to help them successfully engage readers and precisely express meaning. Journalistic writing benefits from well-layered details that help bring problems and solutions into sensory awareness.

Carefully chosen articles with this type of precise and vivid writing help students imagine a setting and prepare them to develop questions that will lead sources to be descriptive. For instance, the July 2019 *Rolling Stone* article "Billie Eilish and the Triumph of the Weird" by Josh Eells packs qualitative details into just two sentences (emphasis added):

> The Eilish home sits on a *leafy* block in L.A.'s Highland Park, a *gentrifying* neighborhood where *discount* party suppliers and *muffler* shops sit alongside cafes and *fancy* pet stores. The two-bedroom bungalow is *cramped and homey*, with *overflowing* bookshelves and, currently, five occupants: Eilish's mom; Eilish's dad; their *rescue* cat, Misha; their *rescue* dog, Pepper; and the biggest, most exciting new pop star of 2019.

It might also be helpful to compare a paragraph like that with one that lacks specificity. For example, this paragraph about a local food pantry, from a hypothetical student, could use some sensory details:

> The food pantry is open every Thursday from 4 p.m. to 6 p.m. during fall, winter, spring and summer terms to all students who show their student ID. Most students find out about the food pantry through posters and social media a bit, or students find out about the pantry through their friends or other programs on campus that tell them about the pantry. The food pantry has a limit to how much food a student can get, one thing from each category.

Next, ask students to examine the mentor text you have chosen in order to find details that measure the characteristics of people, places, and things. Characteristics might include color, type, size, species, position, grade level, gender (for correct pronoun usage), race (used only when relevant), personality traits, or physical traits.

After students find examples in their mentor text, they should look at their

TABLE 5.3   **Qualitative Question Starters**

Ask a source	To get this information
How are you related/connected to _____?	relation to others or organizations
In what city do you live? In what city is your work?	location
What pronouns should we use for you?	gender identity
What type of _____ is _____?	species or category
What does _____ look/smell/sound like?	sensory
How do you feel about _____?	emotional state, opinion
How would you describe _____ (this person or place)?	personality, physical trait
What's the first thing people would notice or comment on about _____ if they visited?	sensory

own questions and notice if they've included those that would lead to specific qualitative details. Table 5.3 lists some qualitative question starters.

Since your students most likely won't be going out to observe situations firsthand, these are details they can gather directly from sources, but only if they think to ask. They also can get creative online, looking at photographs or street views via web-mapping platforms to find visual details of a location important to their topic.

Recognizing the Limits of Quantitative and Qualitative Information

Part of good writing is knowing both the possibilities and the limitations of the details gathered and how to use them in a story. Students should be taught to consider some of the limitations of selecting and incorporating quantitative and qualitative details into their journalistic writing.

First, students may be too eager to use any statistic they find relating to their topic. After all, statistics are a familiar type of quantitative detail that students have likely encountered in other parts of their lives. But statistics are often imperfect. They may come from research that had a small sample size or from a sample that doesn't reflect the entire population it's meant to measure. Sometimes quantitative details or statistics capture information about one aspect of an issue or problem while ignoring other relevant information, creating a distorted view of a topic.

Distortion also can happen if quantitative details—numbers—are isolated from their context. For example, students reporting on school nutrition might discover that one serving of the low-fat chocolate milk served in a school lunch has 25 grams of sugar. At first, they might have no reaction to this specific quantitative detail or even think it's not a big deal. When that detail is put in context with other quantitative information, such as the American Heart Association's recommendation that teenagers consume less than 25 grams of sugar *per day* total, it changes the significance of the data.

In using quantitative details, students should step back to consider if they need to interpret or explain the numbers for readers to clearly understand them. Do they need to give some context? How precise does the context need to be? Depending on the quantitative details students choose to use, this can be a challenge, but if their explanation is done incorrectly, it can misrepresent data. Remind students of their goal: to concisely explain an issue for readers seeking to better understand it. They should know why they are using the numbers they've gathered and how the numbers make the issue clearer to readers.

Qualitative details have limitations, too. One is that they usually cannot be generalized. In other words, writers who observe something in one instance should refrain from suggesting it applies to all instances. For example, if a local food bank has a long line of cars on one Friday afternoon, that doesn't mean the line is long every day. A sentence such as "The food bank draws a crowd every afternoon" may not be true and can, by implication, overestimate the issue of food insecurity in a community. Better to write more specifically: "On a Friday in May, a line of vehicles stretched the length of the food bank's parking lot as people waited for their chance to pick up free groceries."

Numbers and descriptions can be subjective: Students are gathering and sifting through details and choosing only some to include. That's not a bad thing, but it's important for them to consider what is being excluded. How do their choices as writers affect the fairness and accuracy in the story they're writing? Students should be encouraged to remain thoughtful and to create balance between their qualitative and quantitative details. Descriptions can help contextualize numbers, and numbers can help crystallize descriptions. The two types of details cooperate to present a more complete and accurate picture.

Journalistic Skills for Every Career: Project Manager

Project managers plan and oversee an organization's complex collaborative work from start to finish, ensuring that it's completed according to budget and schedule. They frequently write reports that use quantitative and qualitative details to measure performance and track task completion. They also work with public relations and media specialists to help provide the kinds of specific information that will allow outsiders to understand and appreciate the work being done.

Rewording Questions Before the Interview

Questions that invite sources to expound on and explore information in conversation are formulated with forethought. A question asked one way, *Do you think starlings are a problem in our community?* can lead to a truncated, short response: *Yes.* Simply rewording it can make all the difference.

Prior to interviewing sources live, have students spend time shifting from closed-ended to open-ended questions. Questions such as *How much of a problem are starlings for local farmers?* or *What types of problems do starlings create for local farmers?* lead to longer answers, more quotes, and an interview with a conversational feeling.

Give students some closed-ended questions to practice revising to open-ended:

- Is your work challenging? (How challenging is your work?)
- Is this issue getting worse or better? (In what ways is this issue getting worse or better?)
- Are people responding well to recent changes? (How are people responding to recent changes?)
- Do you think this is one of the biggest problems we're facing today? (When considering all the problems we face today, where does this issue fit in importance?)

Additionally, students can practice developing prompting questions on the fly. These are questions reporters ask while listening to a source. Perhaps a source has provided several interesting but brief facts in response to a question. A prompting question might be, *You mentioned* _____ . *Can you say a little more about that?* These types of questions require students to listen carefully and adjust inquiry in the moment based on what they are learning.

Preparing Background and Career Questions for the Interview

There's a fair amount of artifice in the class interviews since often the whole class is observing, rather than just the reporting team that's been researching the issue. The experience is not exactly like an interview that a professional or even scholastic journalist does, nor is it the same experience your class has when with a typical guest speaker. Because it's a novel, hybrid situation, it can be helpful to have students develop background and career questions.

Background questions allow sources to get comfortable in front of the class and hopefully build rapport with young people over shared experiences or places. Background questions are easy for sources; they are used to telling people where they grew up or what their interests and inspirations are. This information also helps students relax, and it can help them become aware of the sometimes-meandering pathways that adults can take to get to where they are.

Background questions might include:

- Where are you from? What was it like to grow up there?
- How did you decide on a path after high school?
- What did you need to do in order to become a _____ ?

Students can then transition to asking sources career questions. These questions may help provide students with context necessary to understand the issue at a deeper level. Career questions also can expose students to careers that may be unfamiliar.

Career questions can include:

- Could you describe your day-to-day work activities?
- What does your job involve?
- What do you like about _____ ?
- What don't you like about _____ ?

Lastly, students should organize the issue questions they've prepared. These might include:

1. 5 Ws and H questions
   - How has _____ changed since you have been involved with it?
   - Why do you think _____ is an important issue for our generation to know about?
   - Who is affected by _____ ?
2. Quantitative questions
   - How many _____ ?
   - What percentage of _____ ?
3. Qualitative questions
   - What does _____ look like when you visit?
   - How would you compare _____ ?
4. Open-ended questions
   - How might people _____ ?
   - What solutions could be possible for _____ ?
5. Present, past, future questions

We recommend reporting teams write 20 to 25 questions for a live interview, with the idea that they may not need to ask them all, or even have the time. Question lists should be prioritized with the most important questions in each category asked first. You might want to have students turn in a complete list of their questions so you can preview them and discuss any concerns or help revise to improve clarity.

Having a backup list on hand for each group also prevents an uncomfortable situation with community members should students misplace their questions or be absent on the day of the interview.

Journalistic Skills for Every Career: Interior Designer

Interior designers interview clients to understand what they would like to do to improve the look and feel of their homes, including furniture placement, window treatments, paint colors, carpet, and more. They employ a standard set of questions in order to get to know a client and help them bring ideas to life. These tend toward open-ended inquiry, such as, "Can you explain how you want to feel when you walk through the front door of your home?" or "How does your family use this room?" They are also skilled at asking in-the-moment prompting questions, such as "Can you tell me more about that?"

CHAPTER 6

Interviewing Community Sources

"They're reaching out all over the world to people who can help them with the story they're writing about."

—9th-Grade English Teacher

THE LIVE INTERVIEW. IT'S at the heart of the journalistic learning approach. It's what students will remember most about their project, even years later.

For young people, it's a chance to step out of their comfort zone and meet adults on a level field to get questions answered. For you, it's a time to sit back and observe from the sidelines while your well-prepared students meet whatever is called for in the moment. Interview days can be exhilarating, fascinating, and unpredictable.

A live interview asks young people to practice the formal communication skills required for many nonschool settings, especially in adulthood. Students accustomed to slouching in their desks or doodling while someone else talks to them will be expected now to shift their body language and posture, to make eye contact, to nod to show understanding, or to give an encouraging smile. For a brief time, they will drop the casual everyday language used with friends and even many teachers in order to engage in a more formal and polite style with a community member.

A 10th-grade instructor explains what she noticed about the interview stage:

I have to admit, I was a little worried that they would be able to pull off a professional style interview. I know how they are with regular interactions. But I noticed how polite they were. I noticed them being really gracious with their guests. I noticed they transitioned really well between topics, and I could tell they had been paying attention as they learned the process leading up to this interview. I felt so proud. I found myself in the back of the room kind of like going "Yes!" Cheering them on. And I knew they were excited.

Interviews build confidence. Being in the interviewer's seat provides students with special insight that they can draw on for future opportunities, such as work, internships, or scholarships. They come to understand, for example, that interviewers are probably a bit nervous. Students experience for themselves just how invested an interviewer is in the conversation going well, maybe even as much as an interviewee.

As you might expect, getting students prepared for interview day takes forethought and careful planning, and this chapter outlines the way. Here we describe how to teach critical interviewing norms in advance, how to give students practice in the interviewer's seat ahead of time, ways to organize your classroom for interview days and how to help students structure their line of inquiry to efficiently cover a lot of ground in a short amount of time.

Anatomy of In-Class Interviews

What do interview days look like? As mentioned in earlier chapters, you will be setting up multiple days of interviews because each reporting team should conduct a live interview. Some teachers organize interviews to run concurrently, either in person or via a video meeting. Student interviews typically run anywhere from 30 to 45 minutes, so the number of interview days you will schedule depends on the number of reporting teams you have and the length of your class periods. Instructors with block schedules of 90 minutes or longer should be able to double up, scheduling two interviews per class session.

Student reporting teams conduct their interviews independently, with as little teacher assistance as possible, using the questions they have prepared and practiced in advance. Classmates can take notes to give to the reporting team afterwards, which allows them the opportunity to practice active listening and real-time note-taking. Each member of the reporting team is expected to ask questions of the source, and the interview is typically recorded, with the permission from the source, so that students can replay it in order to gather accurate quotes for their stories.

Preparing Students for Their Interview

We've found that teaching students a few norms and best practices for before, during, and after their interview can help relieve anxiety and give everyone involved the best chance for a great experience.

In advance of your interview days, we recommend that you provide class time for students to understand and discuss four pre-interview expectations:

1. Source communication
2. Question preparation
3. Attire
4. Unanticipated problems

Interview days can run efficiently or chaotically, and the difference is planning and execution. Building a thoughtful process of communication between sources, students, and you is well worth the time it takes.

Have students remind their sources of the exact time and place of the meeting and get confirmation that they plan to attend. This will help reduce the number of wasted days, when sources don't show up or show up at the wrong time. Reporting teams should check in with sources by writing a polite email or making a phone call a few days in advance, such as:

We are looking forward to meeting you in Room 21 at 11:30 a.m. on Thursday, March 20. You can check in at the front office. Our school address is: 123 School Road.
Thanks so much for taking time to talk with us.

For video appointments:

We are looking forward to speaking by [video conferencing platform] at 11:30 a.m. on Thursday, March 20. Here is the video link: example.url.
Thanks so much for taking time to talk with us.

Once confirmation is made, students should turn their focus to organizing their interview questions. We've found it's a good idea to require them to write questions on paper (or print them out) so that there's a hard copy for interview day. This gives you a chance to review the questions to make sure they are fair and appropriate. It also safeguards against last-minute technical issues, such as the school wireless going down, that might keep students from accessing their questions.

Students can organize their questions in the order that they wish to ask them and assign each question to a member of the reporting team in advance. (Using a clipboard or note cards prevents noisy shuffling of papers during the interview.) Some teams might be tempted to alternate question asking, but we suggest coaching them to divide the interview into sections so that a single reporter is responsible for a section. This helps increase the flow of the interview, making it more conversational.

Students should practice reading each question aloud, so it is clear and sounds natural. Well-prepared students don't sound as though they are reading their questions verbatim, which allows more rapport and eye contact. However, first-time interviewers are not expected to be polished like pros. Nervousness is not only expected but can be endearing and engender trust.

What about sharing questions with sources in advance? It's not typical for professional journalists to do this because reporters want to preserve the ability to ask any question that comes to mind. Journalists also are seeking authentic—not rehearsed—responses. However, community members sometimes inquire ahead of time about the questions students will ask, and you will need to decide in advance what your class response will be so that it's consistent. To be fair, these are not standard interviews, since they may be happening in front of a public audience, with sources who may not have deep personal relationships with the school. Some compromise may be necessary.

If such a request occurs, you might suggest that students provide a general example of questions they will be asking. For example: *We will ask you some questions about the local policy on street camping and ask your opinion about possible solutions.* Reporting teams can reassure the source that they are just learning how to interview and are not attempting to engage in any sort of gotcha journalism.

You might wish to give students guidelines and examples about what to wear for their interview. Journalists who aren't on camera are not typically known for being very fashion forward at work. When they're not hunched over a computer typing up stories, their job often requires racing through traffic from one place to another, working in extreme weather, or standing for a long time while waiting for updates. However, reporters usually follow a business casual code of professional dress. This may vary based on your school culture.

Finally, prior to their interviews, students should anticipate some of the problems that might arise at the last minute. For example:

- What if one member of the reporting team is absent?
- What if our questions get lost?
- What if our source is late and our time runs short?

Ask reporting teams to think through and discuss these scenarios and prepare. *Which of the problems do you think your team may be most likely to face, and how will you avoid or handle it? Are there any other predicaments you can anticipate?* Follow up with a class discussion so everyone can hear the range of problems and solutions.

Preparation pays dividends, as one 11th-grade teacher discovered:

> I told my students I was nervous for them, concerned because they'd been so scared during their practice interviews. But they actually, like every single one of them, had everything organized. Even down to "Who's going to say hello?" "Who's going to take over next?" "What order are we going in?" I think my students have done a really good job.

Interview Day Norms

We recommend teaching and allowing time for students to discuss or practice seven interview day norms:

1. Arrival times
2. Appreciation of the source
3. Permission to record
4. Reminder of the story angle
5. Adapting to more formal speaking
6. Positive body language
7. Active listening techniques

Students should plan to arrive on time for their interviews, and by "on time," we advise early. For an in-person interview, arriving at the meeting place about five minutes early is a good habit to help students build. This usually assures a source isn't standing around waiting, but rather is greeted the moment they arrive. For an online video interview, we recommend students get into the virtual meeting room at least two minutes early so a source is greeted shortly after they log on. For a phone interview, students should make the call or be ready to receive the call on the dot.

If the source is coming to the school in person, you might have your students meet them in the school office to walk them to the classroom. Encourage students to shake hands and make eye contact. This simple gesture helps establish rapport. It also allows for less formal introductions and some casual chitchat while walking across campus—an excellent way to help sources and students get to know each other and feel more comfortable from the start.

Students can begin the interview by introducing the source to the class, followed by a reminder of their names and a brief acknowledgement of the source's time. A simple opening might be practiced in advance:

(*To class:*) "This is Ms. _____ who serves as a _____." (*To source:*) "My name is _____ and this is _____ and _____. Thank you so much for meeting with us today for this interview."

If your students will be recording the interview in order to access it later, they should ask the source if it's okay if they record. State laws vary for obtaining consent to record a conversation, and the rules are changing in some states as new technologies develop. As of 2022, 37 states and the District of Columbia allow what's known as "one-party consent." This means only one side needs to be aware of the recording.

At the time of this writing, 13 states have "two-party consent" laws, requiring both parties to know about and agree to the recording: California, Connecticut (for remote recording only), Delaware, Florida, Hawaii (for remote recording where the recorder is not visible), Illinois, Maryland, Massachusetts, Montana, New Hampshire, Oregon (for in-person recording only), Pennsylvania, and Washington.

No matter what your state law is, we encourage all students to ask permission to record their sources so that reporting teams can play the interviews back later. If sources seem uncertain about being recorded, students can let them know how the recording will be used. In most cases, this likely means students will replay the interview and listen for exact quotes to ensure accuracy. If students want to use audio or video elements from a recorded interview to make a multimedia supplement for their written article, sources should be informed of that.

Once introductions and requests to record are out of the way, it's a good idea for students to introduce the topic of their research and share the scope of questions they will be asking. This provides structure for the interview while reminding the source and the class about what to expect for the next half hour or so.

An introduction might sound like this:

> For the past few weeks, we've been looking into the types of resources our community provides for families who are experiencing food insecurity. We're interested in finding out how your work connects to this issue. We'd like to start with questions about your background and career and then ask you more specifically about food insecurity in our town, if that's okay?

As all English teachers who have assigned students formal presentations are aware, it's important to coach basic public speaking norms, including three that we suggest you highlight:

1. Voice projection and speed
2. Avoiding slang
3. Avoiding jokes

Even quiet classrooms can be noisy when dozens of students sit in proximity, especially when air conditioners or furnaces are running. Typical noises like shuffling notebook paper, clicking binders, dropped pencils, tapping feet, creaking chairs, and all the outside ambient sounds add up. Combined with student shyness, sources may have difficulty hearing questions the first time, so coach students to speak up and project their voices to be more easily heard.

Students also need to remember that their sources probably haven't seen or heard their interview questions beforehand, so they will have to work harder to comprehend and process them. Speaking clearly and a bit more slowly than normal should be practiced.

Depending on your classroom culture, it may be a good idea to discuss why everyday slang and joking around are inappropriate for interview day. Adults may find student slang a bit confusing, particularly if they aren't parents of teenagers or don't often work around youth. Slang can make guests uneasy or uncertain in the formal interview. Jokes that often bring welcome humor to an ordinary classroom day among people who know each other well can be misinterpreted and backfire with outsiders and might even suggest students aren't taking their research—or the source's time and expertise—seriously.

Nonverbal norms can also signify respect for the source and attention during the interview process. Such body language often includes sitting or standing up straight, smiling occasionally, and keeping arms relaxed, not in pockets or crossed. Students should indicate active listening with eye contact and by occasionally nodding affirmatively from time to time as the source makes a point.

Interviewers also might use brief verbal affirmations to give their source encouragement or to signal a transition:

- "I see."
- "That's interesting and very helpful!"
- "Thank you. Our next question is . . . "

Some or all of these verbal and nonverbal indicators that traditionally indicate respect and attention in formal or professional settings in the United States may not feel comfortable or be intuitive for neurodivergent students. In addition to preparing questions and sending reminder emails to sources, teachers may find it helpful to spend some time explicitly teaching verbal and nonverbal cues and having students practice them during mock and peer interviews.

Organizing Mock and Peer Practice Interviews

Taking a class period to engage students with a mock interview is one of the best ways to help them prepare. The mock interview can be any of the following that you arrange in advance:

- You interview a campus adult (assistant principal, counselor, support staff)
- A volunteer student interviews a campus adult
- You interview a volunteer student
- A volunteer student interviews a peer

A mock interview can be impromptu, with questions structured to mirror the upcoming student interviews.

If interviewing a campus adult, consider asking:

- Background: *Please tell me about where and when you grew up. What were middle and high school like for you? What was your path like after high school?*
- Career: *How long have you been a _____? What are the requirements for this job in terms of education or licensing? Please describe a typical day or week in your job.*
- Issue: *What do you think is the biggest challenge in your work today? What are some of the solutions to problems that you would like to see?*
- Follow-up questions: *I'd like to follow up on what you said about _____; please tell me more about that. I didn't quite understand what you said about _____; please explain it again.*

If interviewing a student, consider asking:

- Background: *Please describe where you grew up and what you were like as a kid. What is one of your top memories about our community that you might like to remember for the rest of your life?*
- School: *Please tell me about your favorite class or project in school, either past or present. What advice would you give younger students about this grade level, in terms of homework or staying on top of grades or stress?*
- Issue: *Of all the challenges or problems in the world today, which one do you*

spend more time thinking about? What connection does this problem have to your friends and family, if any? How would life change if this problem was solved?

- Follow-up questions: *I'd like to follow up on what you said about* _____ *; please tell me more about that. I didn't quite understand what you said about* _____ *; please explain it again.*

After the mock interview, discuss with students what they observed. *What did you notice about how I* _____ *? How do you know that this interview can be considered a success?*

Model genuine engagement for students by expressing appreciation for any discoveries. *"I never knew that* _____ *"* or *"I was fascinated when she talked about* _____ *."* Focusing on the new insights gained will help students understand a critical point about their upcoming interviews: they are a means to a goal, not the goal itself.

This is the time to tell your students the truth about interviews. None of them go perfectly. Even professional journalists with many years of experience fumble or experience awkward moments. Any interview—whether for school or work—tends to cause each of us to consider afterwards, sometimes with a bit of regret: *I wish I had . . .*

This is natural and to be expected. The best we can do is prepare adequately, try to recover from missteps in the moment, and then let it go. Human communication is simply unpredictable, which makes it interesting.

After the mock interview, a quick peer-to-peer interview helps students practice. Ask students to break into pairs with someone from a different reporting team or someone they don't know well. Offer two topic choices, such as:

1. An unexpected situation you experienced as a kid
2. A favorite place to eat with friends or family

Then project some sample questions that they can practice asking each other:

- Please tell me a little about yourself, where you grew up and what you like to do.
- Please describe . . . (a situation that really stressed you out as a kid) or (your favorite place to eat).
- I'd like to follow up on what you said about _____ ; please tell me more about that.

- I didn't quite understand what you said about _____.
  Please explain it again.

Direct students to add whatever new questions they like in the moment so that their source is encouraged to go into more detail. Afterwards, ask students to consider: *What went well? What will you do differently next time?*

Providing an Interview Checklist

Giving students a checklist helps ease their nerves in two ways. First, it crystallizes some conceptual boundaries of the interview—capturing expectations on paper where they are easy to review or discuss. Anxiety over public speaking can diminish by seeing exactly what is expected.

Second, a checklist can serve as a postinterview tool for students to use as they self-reflect: *How do you think you did? What exactly was hard or easy? What specifically would you work on for next time?*

Teachers might wish to introduce a checklist like the sample checklist in Table 6.1 prior to the mock or peer interviews so the class has a chance to discuss each category.

TABLE 6.1   Interview Expectations Checklist

Interview Checklist					
Prep	Remind source of the interview time and location	Prepare all questions, including the order and who will ask each one	Plan what to wear	Plan for contingencies: • if a team member is absent • if questions get lost • if source is late and you have less time	Arrive on time, which means early
Interview Structure	Introduce yourselves to source	Adapt your speech to be more formal, polite	Show appreciation for the opportunity	Ask permission to record	Explain story angle before asking questions
Active Listening	Make eye contact	Nod	Keep arms open	Use good posture	
Types of Questions	Ask quantitative questions	Ask qualitative questions	Ask open-ended questions	Ask follow-up questions	

Staging the Interview Day

It's a good idea to plan your classroom arrangement in advance of the first interview so that you achieve the best conditions for the guest and your students. It works well to have the source sit on a chair with good height, such as a director's chair or a bar stool, so that all students can see and hear well. Reporting teams can sit up front in student chairs, which should prevent unnecessary fidgeting or shuffling that can happen when students stand together. Some teachers like to do a fishbowl arrangement, with sources and reporting teams in the middle of a circle of observers.

With video interviews, you might choose to stage the room in a way that is consistent with in-person interviews out of respect for the student journalists and so that it doesn't feel to other students less important than in-person interviews or like a free day, when they don't have to pay much attention. Projecting the interview on a big screen and playing audio through a strong speaker is ideal.

Working out the recording process in advance is essential. Depending on the age and abilities of your students, this might mean one of the student reporters uses a voice recorder app on their cell phone, which is what professional journalists typically do. Or it might mean using a class computer to record. If one or more interviews will take place via videoconferencing, ensure the software you use has a record function. Have students decide which of them will be responsible for pressing the record button after getting source permission.

Time is always a consideration. If you are squeezing two interviews into a block period, students will need to be able to transition quickly from one guest to the next. Even in a single period, someone in each reporting team needs to keep an eye on the clock so that the most important questions have a chance to be asked before class is over.

The challenge for students is that they cannot know in advance how long it will take for their source to answer each question. Some sources are natural storytellers and will go on and on, while others are succinct, and the interview may speed by in what feels like a few minutes. If there is time left after the last question, reporting teams can ask student note-takers if they have additional questions. They shouldn't interrupt an interview with their own questions, however, since it's the reporting team's moment to lead.

What are the other students doing during the interview? We recommend they practice note-taking on paper. We advise against digital note-taking because of how distracting computers can be and because guests may not be accustomed to speaking to a group of people who are clicking away on keyboards. Paper notes are easy to collect immediately after the interview and give to the reporting team.

You might suggest note-takers listen for three quotable statements from the source and try to write them down word for word, if they can. Students can also be prompted to write down any mention of quantitative details or statistics. Ask them to note the part of the interview they found most interesting and one thing they'd like to learn more about, both of which can help the reporters understand what others find most compelling about the topic.

What about you? We encourage you to turn over the entire process of the interview to the students. Help facilitate only if the interview is at risk of ending prematurely or if there is peer conflict or a technology problem. We recommend not stepping in to smooth over awkward pauses or to clarify what the students might have intended to ask or know. It's hard not to interject, but any success or failure during the interview must be theirs and theirs alone. It's the independence that builds confidence, improvisation, and social–emotional resiliency.

Letting students sink or swim in the moment also signals to the rest of the class a high degree of teacher confidence. The improvement between the first interviews and the last can be profound when the instructor steps aside and allows students to learn from each other, as one high school teacher learned the first time she taught the project:

> Talking to real people as part of research makes that real-world connection. They're thinking of this problem academically and talking to somebody who's an expert about it. And sometimes they have had some of their preconceived notions picked apart. They've had to kind of rethink actually what they thought was true. For example, I've learned a lot about how little some of the students know about how local government works. (A source will say) "this is my jurisdiction, and this is somebody else's jurisdiction. This is what I'm in charge of, and this is what I'm not in charge of." It's been a good lesson for them, civically, but also just on a personal level.

Sitting back to let your students lead frees you to observe each interview and provide notes to the reporting teams about what you notice. Your notes might be aligned to listening and speaking skills that you feel are most necessary for students to master, or to your state or district standards, or they might be related to the interview criteria you have given students in advance, such as those in the checklist we outlined in the previous section.

You can use your notes to inform any later evaluations, as well. This is the time to give students concise constructive and immediate feedback while the experience is fresh:

- I observed these strengths:
- I saw these areas for future growth:
- Next time, try to:

After the Interview: What's Next?

Once the interview ends, the source should be thanked and escorted back to the office. Student note-takers should turn in their notes, either to the instructor or directly to the reporting team. If time permits, you might wish to debrief as a class after the interview. This helps other students make essential adjustments before it's their turn and can help the interviews get better each day.

Three or four debriefing questions are plenty:

1. What worked well?
2. What could have gone better?
3. How do the reporters feel now that it's over?
4. What did the source say that you will remember most from this interview?

We are big believers in student reflection and self-assessment. Both support metacognitive growth and are valuable as formative assessment practices. If you're new to self-evaluation tools, keep in mind when asking students to think about their thinking that it's most valuable as a formative, not a summative, assessment. Self-evaluation should be used to gauge learning and improve work prior to grading, not necessarily as a grade.

In order to build student confidence and increase awareness for future interviews, self-assessment requires clear instruction, modeling, and criteria. One way to do this is to ask students to process and reflect on their interview experience in writing. Have them do this as soon as possible after their interview, while motivation is high, so the details do not get fuzzy or forgotten. They can write a narrative about how it went.

You might use or adapt a prompt such as:

Write about how your interview went and how you feel now that it's over. Then, using criteria from the interview checklist, describe at least one strength (your own or your team's) and one growth area in each category.

For many people, public speaking—much less conducting an interview with a stranger in front of their peers—is legitimately frightening. Written reflections will give you insight into how your students are feeling and whether you may need to meet with them to debrief in private.

Guiding Students to Follow Up

Within 24 hours of the interview, we recommend that reporting teams write a brief thank you and pose a couple of follow-up questions by emailing their source, noting specific parts of the interview that were especially interesting or helpful. This thoughtful act is a nice way to help sources feel a sense of closure. It creates a feeling of community and goodwill, making it more likely they will agree to return in following years and to spread the word about the kind of work students are doing in your class.

A quick thank you email is an ideal opportunity to pose one or two follow-up questions, and we encourage students to think of some. Perhaps there are some quantitative details that the source alluded to but didn't have specifics for at the moment. Or possibly they mentioned the name of someone else in the field to whom students could reach out.

Follow-up questions should be limited to a couple and should be connected to some part of the interview; they should not introduce a whole new line of inquiry. The key is to be brief:

> *We want to express our appreciation for the time you gave us today. It was so help-ful. We especially liked the information you provided about _____.*
> *We have two follow-up questions that would be beneficial for our story.*
> *First, _____*
> *Second, _____*
> *Thanks again!*

This is also a good time to check back in with reporting teams to see if they need assistance. Perhaps the source didn't give them the information they were hoping for. Perhaps new information from the interview is taking them in a different direction and they feel muddled. There may be a bit more research needed, and they may need to talk it out with you to get back on track for the next stage: writing their articles.

Journalistic Skills for Every Career: Salesperson

Appliance, furniture, and auto salespeople use active listening and questioning techniques to understand a customer's specific needs. There are so many variables to consider when buying a car, washing machine, or sofa, including size, style, how it will be used, budget, and personal tastes. A practiced salesperson understands how to make someone they've just met feel comfortable sharing personal details so they can help match them with the right product.

CHAPTER 7

Writing Their Story

"I think that the students are starting to feel both excited and a sense of accountability, that they're going to be writing something that people are going to see."

—High School English Teacher

FOR LANGUAGE ARTS TEACHERS, the writing stage of a journalistic learning project may be at once familiar and foreign. Familiar because it mirrors some traditional scholastic writing patterns that you recognize, with students moving from draft to peer review to revision. A bit foreign because you may never have assigned writing for the purpose of publication—or written for a publication yourself—and aren't exactly sure what to expect from your students.

Like teaching any other lengthy essay, this is the point where you will watch some of your students shift almost effortlessly or naturally into producing well-organized and interesting, informative articles with minimal help, like ducks to water. They paddle off in the direction of wherever they want to go. But this is also a time when you might notice that other students have little idea of what to do and are set to flail about, spin in circles, or even shut down unless they get clear directions and support.

We have known for a long time that American students struggle to write well. Only 24% of U.S. 8th- and 12th-graders scored proficient in writing on the 2011 National Assessment of Educational Progress test (National Center for Education Statistics, 2012), the most recent national bank of scores we have, since the NAEP is not tested annually in many states. Your state or school standardized writing scores may look similarly bleak.

There are many reasons for the low performance, which we won't address here beyond stating that teaching writing is one of the most challenging responsibilities on the language arts teacher's very crowded plate. With total student loads increasing and chronic absences skyrocketing since 2020, English teachers—no matter how great they are at teaching writing—simply do not have adequate time to provide enough individual support and feedback.

It may be tempting at this point of the project to look around and question your sanity. *What was I thinking? Should I assign a quick write and move on to our next unit?*

After all, so much has already been introduced and achieved: news literacy skills, inquiry and interview strategies, real-world experience speaking professionally with adults. *The kids have come so far, and don't we want to end the project on a high note?*

We get it. But we strongly encourage you to devote substantive class time to the writing and revision part of this project and to the creation of scholastic news articles for publication. For one thing, it might be easier than you imagine to rally your students. We've found that writers who anticipate their work being published for a wide audience feel a sense of empowerment, and this may motivate your class to work with more clarity and motivation than they do on traditional academic essays.

It's true, too, that journalistic writing is transactional: actual readers might be willing to give up some of their valuable attention in exchange for important information. Students who learn to write journalistically often evolve as writers, in part because they learn to consider two simple questions: *Who am I writing for? How can I connect with them?*

Journalism is a noble service, and students may be persuaded to feel a sense of responsibility that is novel and energizing. Sprinkling the phrase "your future readers" throughout your instruction from this point on will help reinforce the idea.

Additionally, practice with journalistic writing prepares students for other types of real-world writing. College application essays use the same storytelling techniques that journalistic articles use, including gripping hooks and colorful quotations. Business summaries rely on short, swift-moving paragraphs and succinct details.

Journalistic writing even helps fiction writers and poets. Many notable American literary authors started as journalists, including Maya Angelou, Hanya Yanagihara, Langston Hughes, Joan Didion, Ernest Hemingway, Daniel Alarcón, John Steinbeck, Mark Twain, and Ta-Nehisi Coates.

In this chapter, we'll explain how to help your students craft their articles, from knowing how to start and end, to finding the right order for the information they've gathered, to quoting sources with proper attribution. We'll present examples of how you can guide your students to plug informational holes or eliminate unnecessary repetition. And we'll give you a set of insider style rules that introduce them to Associated Press style.

Organizing Students to Write

Your students have been working in small reporting teams for most of the project so far, and you will need to decide by this stage what proportion of the finished news article each student will be responsible for drafting. Some teachers find it works well to have student groups decide for themselves if they want to either divvy up the writing or collaboratively draft the entire article. Other instructors like to decide what to require.

One high school teacher has her reporting teams cowrite a lede and a closing together, then has reporting teams divide the middle into thirds or fourths so that each student writes 500 to 700 words of the article. Other teachers say they prefer to have every student write their own article, from start to finish, using shared notes.

No matter what structure you go with, your students will feel more comfortable if expectations are clear. Consider creating a writing criteria sheet (or cocreating it with students) that includes the following:

- Total minimum word count, or range, for the article
- Collaborative writing tasks (ledes, closings, etc.)
- Individual writing tasks (with minimum word counts or ranges)
- News writing elements (e.g., minimum number of quantitative and qualitative details, direct quotations and source attributions, etc.)
- Number of drafts you expect to be turned in (may also include outlines, notes, etc.)
- Deadlines

Students should by now have an abundance of notes from online secondary sources and primary sources they have interviewed. It's helpful to have them get everything out and simply go through what they have.

We suggest asking them to work together to prioritize the information, organizing it into details about the past, present, and future. Transcripts or notes from oral interviews can be cut up and organized into three areas, as can any notes from online research. The work of sorting often leads naturally to discussing and deciding who will write what.

Outlining Before Drafting

Some teachers believe it essential for students to create outlines before starting to write, and we tend to agree that this will help prevent inadvertent holes, unnecessary repetition, and confusion down the road when the sections are patched together to form the whole.

A simple bullet outline can work well, and you might provide students with an example of one from the mentor text you've chosen to use. (Yes, the mentor text will still be used throughout the writing process, and it is normal for students to roll their eyes and complain at having to consider it yet again. Trust us, using the same text at this stage saves much time.)

Figure 7.1 offers an example of a simple outline based on the "Starlings" article that we've been examining throughout this book. Students should be able to imagine that the writer, Megan Banta, sat down after her interviews and research, looked through her notes and quickly organized a plan.

Be sure to encourage students to describe their issue from multiple viewpoints, possibly even including how issues impact animals, plants, or ecosystems. They should discuss and carefully choose who to give the first quote to, since this person's thoughts will introduce the angle of the story and impact readers more than someone quoted near the end of the piece.

Banta chose to give the first quote about starlings to the professor who studies dairy farms, for example: "There's just so many of them, and they're kind of voracious eaters." This perspective is factual and not opinionated, and it introduces two of the reasons the starlings have become a problem.

Have students compare a hypothetical pre-draft outline with the article so they can understand there is no specific template or formula for journalistic writing. For example, they won't write one paragraph per bullet point, but rather, as Banta did, they'll write as many paragraphs as they need to convey information. Likewise, there's no rule for how many words or sentences are in a journalistic article. (Traditionally, the paragraphs are very short, often only one or two sentences long, which helps readers breeze through the text.)

A quick outline allows writers to get a sense of the scope of their article without feeling boxed in. As they write, they have freedom to make nuanced writing decisions, such as where quantitative details fit or which quotation works.

It shouldn't take more than a class period for reporting teams to collaborate on an outline and decide who will take on each part of the article. Once these

FIGURE 7.1   **Before beginning to write their articles, students can organize information from research and interviews into a simple past–present–future bullet outline.**

Working Title: The Pros and Cons of Starlings in Eugene

Lede: Setting Up the Problem
- Hint why starlings are pests
  - Farmer's viewpoint
- Hint why starlings are beneficial
  - Academic's viewpoint
- Hint what to do about them

Past: Explain why Things Got This Way
- History of starlings in the area
  - Appearance of birds
  - Introduction to the United States
  - Introduction to Oregon

Present: Explain Both Sides of the Issue Today
- Starling harm
  - Farm damage
  - Urban annoyance
- Starling benefits
  - Examine prejudices
  - Beauty
  - Birder's viewpoint

Future: Actions People Can Take
- Farmer's advice
- Academic's advice
- Landfill employee's advice

Credit: The Journalistic Learning Initiative

decisions have been agreed upon, it's time to look at what works to catch a reader's attention: a great lede.

Writing a Journalistic Lede

Hooking a reader with clear, compelling, and succinct writing is a journalistic skill that transfers. Whether it's an email, a memo, an invitation, a request, or a summary, writing should start by catching someone's interest.

In traditional academic writing, the beginning of an essay or story is called a hook. In journalistic writing, it's called a lede and is simply the opening sentences or paragraphs of a news article. The lede describes the most important aspects of the story and indicates an angle or approach by which to understand the information to come.

Ledes vary greatly in structure and length. Some are a single line. Others, such as those used for feature length articles, might be five or six grafs (spelled this way by journalists as a shorthand for paragraphs and to distinguish it from a mathematical graph that might be included in an article showing quantitative information).

Traditionally, ledes were short because printed news was expensive to publish. In digital publications, this is not an issue, so there is no set rule for how long a lede should be. The key is to hold a reader's attention long enough to get them invested in the story.

We recommend that you have your students examine the lede in the mentor text. Ask them to determine how long it is and note the following:

- How many sources are mentioned in the lede?
- How many quotes are included?
- Does the lede include the 5 Ws and H information for readers?
- How many quantitative details are in it?
- Are there many or few qualitative details in it?
- Count the sentences in the lede. What do you notice?

With the "Starlings" article, we ask students to examine the first six paragraphs:

As employees at Short Mountain Landfill maneuver heavy machinery to compact trash, a throng of birds lifts and swarms before settling back down on the garbage.

The birds aren't seagulls, ravens, crows or magpies — all of which are common at landfills.

They're European starlings.

An invasive species, starlings closely resemble blackbirds and often draw the ire of many birders, farmers and others because they can pose a threat to native bird species and crops. Invasive species are living organisms that are not native to an ecosystem and cause harm.

On farms, starlings are most noticeable among the pest birds, said Jenifer Cruikshank, who works for the Oregon State University Extension Service focusing on dairy farms.

"There's just so many of them, and they're kind of voracious eaters," she said.

Banta's lede sets up the problem and introduces one of the sources using a direct quote. It swiftly answers most of the basic 5 Ws and H questions:

- What is the problem? (*They are a threat to native species, crops, and local ecosystems*)
- Who is affected? (*Birders, farmers, and others*)
- Where is the problem presenting itself? (*Not stated directly, but uses Oregon source*)
- When did it start? (*Not stated in lede*)
- Why is this important? (*Harm is being caused*)
- How are people affected? (*Not stated directly but we can infer crops and native species are being negatively impacted*)

Banta's lede is not weighed down with numbers, statistics, or heavy quotes from sources. She saves the quantitative details for later. Instead, she focuses on the more easily absorbed qualitative details with precise visual description:

"employees at Short Mountain Landfill maneuver heavy machinery"
"a throng of birds lifts and swarms"
"birds aren't seagulls, ravens, crows, or magpies"
"closely resemble blackbirds"

Notice how short and skinny Banta's paragraphs are, each just one sentence. This choice allows readers to fly through her lede and feel a sense of ease as they absorb the parameters of the starling problem.

Giving students a lede scaffold is also helpful. The "Starlings" article is illustrative of lede structure, as shown in Figure 7.2. You might suggest they use this format to open their article:

- Describe a setting
- Describe the problem
- Quote from a source

Students may wonder how they can describe a setting if they haven't been there in person. One idea is to email a source to ask for visual and auditory (or even olfactory) descriptions. Another idea, at least if the setting is outside and on a public street, is looking at an online map. Street or satellite views available in online maps can offer general visual details. Some students may be motivated to visit one or more settings on their own time after class too.

Creating swift-moving ledes using lively descriptions and quotes is a challenge, and even professional journalists feel stumped sometimes. Some of the

FIGURE 7.2   **Examine a strong lede from a mentor text to help students understand how they might begin their articles by efficiently packing facts and source opinion into the opening paragraphs.**

Lede Structure

Describe a setting where your issue has been observed recently, either directly by you or as described by a source who has been there.

Describe how the issue is a problem for people, animals, ecosystems, etc.

Add a direct quote from a source, who describes the problem in their own words.

As employees at Short Mountain Landfill maneuver heavy machinery to compact trash, a throng of birds lifts and swarms before settling back down on the garbabge.

The birds aren't seagulls, ravens, crows or magpies—all of which are common at landfills.

They're European starlings.

An invasive species, starlings closely resemble blackbirds and often draw the ire of many birders, farmers and others because they can pose a threat to native bird species and crops. Invasive species are living organisms that are not native to an ecosystem and cause harm.

On farms, starlings are most noticeable among the pest birds, said Jenifer Cruikshank, who works for the Oregon State University Extension Srevice focusing on dairy farms.

"There's just so many of them, and they're kind of voracious eaters," she said.

Excerpted from the article "Starlings in Oregon are an invasive pest to some, a fascinating species facing 'bio bigotry' to others," by Megan Banta, *The Eugene Register-Guard*

Credit: The Journalistic Learning Initiative

pros will write a sloppy placeholder lede until they finish the article and then go back and rewrite the opening later when they have more clarity. If your students are spending a lot of time and getting frustrated trying to write the perfect lede, you can suggest this option to them.

Quoting Primary Sources

Quotes from primary-source interviews give journalistic stories a sense of immediacy and personality, bringing individual voices into conversation with each other. A source is speaking for themselves, directly to readers, having chosen their own words.

Students may be familiar with using quotations in a narrative story, where characters talk to each other through dialogue. They are likely also familiar with citing secondary sources in formal academic essays. They probably have not written journalistically, so integrating full and partial quotes from interviews into their factual articles may be new.

Professional journalists take great care to accurately quote and attribute the information they use, whether it has been personally gathered or taken from previously published works. They are responsible for making sure quoted information is presented in context and with balance, using proper attribution so that it can be traced to the source if there are questions or concerns. Journalists use quotes from sources with restraint—as one would hot sauce.

It's a good idea to teach students how to use both full quotes and partial quotes. A full quote—a complete sentence from a source—makes sense when it stands alone. It is already grammatically correct and succinct and is often colorful, showing emotion or creating a vivid picture or offering a compelling opinion.

This quote about a hypothetical incident in a school cafeteria fits the bill:

"Food was all over the place, and the floor was a slimy mess," she said. "The custodians were pretty dismayed, to be honest."

A partial quote—a word or phrase pulled from an interview—is integrated into the writer's own sentence. Journalists use partial quotes if a source's sentence is too long or is grammatically incorrect (which often happens when people talk, and journalists try to avoid making their sources sound dim-witted). A partial quote gets to the heart of a statement, providing a pop of color or interest.

Journalists use partial quotes in the same context and with the same intended meaning as their source. For example:

The food fight left "a slimy mess" on the cafeteria floor, she said.

One mistake novice writers tend to make when integrating quotes into their descriptive paragraphs is inadvertently repeating details. They write the same information twice, once in the setup for the quote and then again in the quote itself.

Here's an example of unnecessarily repeated details:

The food fight left food everywhere, especially the floor, upsetting school custodians.

"Food was all over the place, and the floor was a slimy mess," she said. "The custodians were pretty dismayed, to be honest."

Solving this issue means working backwards. Choose a good quote and then carefully build a paragraph that transitions to it by offering some context without giving away what the source will be saying. For example:

The impact of student food fights on school staff is serious, both in terms of increased labor and a sense of disrespect, said the cafeteria manager.

"Food was all over the place, and the floor was a slimy mess," she said. "The custodians were pretty dismayed, to be honest."

Attribution is critical for quotations, and there is a format that journalists follow: *"Full Quote," Name said.* For example:

"Food was all over the place, and the floor was a slimy mess. The custodians were pretty dismayed, to be honest," Principal Maria Villegas said.

Typically, full names of sources are used only on first mention, followed by just the last name or a pronoun for following mentions. A source's relationship to the issue should also be provided on the first reference.

Punctuation follows the typical rule for American English. Place commas or periods inside the quote marks. Use a period after the word "said."

Notice repetition of the word "said" in these examples. Students who have lots of quotes may feel that "said" gets too repetitive and want to substitute *exclaimed*, *uttered*, or *declared*. However, these words, while used often in fiction writing, can unwittingly change the tone of the source's statement. Because of this, we (and the professionals) recommend sticking with "said" for the entire piece.

Paraphrasing Primary Sources

The ability to paraphrase information to make it easier to understand or faster to absorb is one of the key skills honed by journalistic writing. The goal is to offer a smooth and fast reading experience.

To help students understand the power of paraphrasing, the class can examine the mentor text you have chosen. Ask students to notice the balance between paraphrased information and quoted material.

For example, in the "Starlings" article, we see this breakdown:

- Total paragraphs: 58
- Paragraphs that contain a full quote: 6
- Paragraphs that contain a partial quote: 6
- Proportion of paragraphs with any quote: 20%
- Proportion of paragraphs with only paraphrased information: 80%

An article with too many quotes will be tough to read and probably lack enough context. An article with too much paraphrasing will seem less relatable and more like a summary of secondary sources. An 80 to 20 proportion of paraphrasing to quotes seems about right.

Your students may not be sure what paraphrasing is, or how it works, so it can be helpful to look at a hypothetical interview (or a transcript of an actual interview) and practice turning a bit of it into journalistic writing.

Here, a hypothetical city engineer was interviewed about pandemic-related traffic:

Question: *When did the traffic problem downtown start, and what do you think is causing it?*

Answer: "We started getting a lot of complaints last summer. The pandemic caused restaurants to either shut down or operate outside, and it was, uh, not a last-minute decision necessarily, but I guess you could say it was the city's effort to try to help them stay alive for an indefinite amount of time. We blocked off Main Street between Oak and Fir . . . no cars allowed, pedestrians only, for the first time ever in the history of the city, since horse and wagon days. This let the restaurants set up tables in the street. Social distanced tables. And we got a lot of positive feedback. Restaurants not only survived, the whole downtown started attracting more foot traffic, so much so that we won't be opening up Main Street to cars any time soon. Lots more tourists coming from out of town . . . very positive. Unfortunately, the cars—hundreds more—started using Santa Clara and Poli streets."

Here's how a young writer might paraphrase the excerpt, condensing the information to its essence:

The traffic downtown has become an issue for some residents since last summer. That's when the pandemic caused city officials to try something for the first time: No cars on Main Street between Oak and Fir streets.

This historic change allowed restaurants to place tables out on the sidewalk and into the street for safer dining and has been a hit with "lots more tourists coming from out of town," city traffic engineer Maris Ensari said.

Not everything needs attribution. The rule is basically this: general information that is commonly or widely known does not need a source. For instance, a commonly known detail such as "the cafeteria is next to the gym" needs no attribution.

Specific information that is not widely known by a general readership typically does need attribution. For example:

> "The cafeteria was closed the next day, which caused students to eat out in the drizzling rain, said the cafeteria manager."

Crediting Secondary Sources

Most students will be relying on multiple secondary sources for their stories in addition to their primary source interviews. These might include information gathered online from published articles, research papers, videos, or podcasts. Crediting these sources is both necessary and straightforward.

For example, say your students want to include information from an article they found online about unhoused residents, in this case a news feature titled "Eugene 'bailing out Titanic with a teacup' helping people living in vehicles and addressing impacts," which also happens to have been written by *The Register-Guard*'s Megan Banta (2022). They might paraphrase facts from the article and use a direct quote, attributing the information like this:

> The pandemic created tension between people living in their vehicles and residents who work and live in those neighborhoods. According to an article in *The Register-Guard* in April, police requests related to people living in their cars hit a peak in June 2021 with 1,283 requests for assistance, more than tripling from March 2020.
>
> "It sometimes feels like we're bailing out the Titanic with a teacup. We need bigger, bolder solutions," Eugene City Councilor Randy Groves told *The Register-Guard*.

News stories do not have a bibliography and do not generally name the authors or titles of secondary sources unless they are well known or particularly pertinent to the subject matter.

What About Anonymous Sources and Pseudonyms?

Sources sometimes share private information to which they do not wish to be publicly connected, and journalists take care to establish parameters in advance. For stories involving substance abuse or mental illness, for example, reporters often agree to use a pseudonym to allow the source to speak with confidentiality.

The Society of Professional Journalists (SPJ; 2014) Code of Ethics (SPJ; 2014) offers guidance:

> Consider sources' motives before promising anonymity. Reserve anonymity for sources who may face danger, retribution or other harm, and have information that cannot be obtained elsewhere. Explain why anonymity was granted.

The National Scholastic Press Association encourages full transparency when pseudonyms are used (Hiestand, n.d.):

> Readers must be informed. A prominent disclaimer at the top of the story explaining that names (and any other details) have been changed is a must. Not only do ethics demand that readers not be misled, a disclaimer also provides protection against claims that a party has been wrongly identified.

Students who wish to use a pseudonym for a source should also be aware of their responsibility to protect the source by not divulging their name to classmates, friends, or family members in casual discussion prior to or after publication.

Balancing Quotes to Show the Complexity of an Issue

Students have already learned the ethical reasons to try to set aside their own assumptions and biases while researching an issue, and they should work hard to present their stories fairly to allow readers to form their own opinions. Remind students to present information from as many sides as they can, and especially to not allow one source to dominate by getting all the quotes.

We suggest you guide students to examine the mentor text you have been using to count how many times each source is mentioned. For example, in the "Starlings" article, we can see how many times each of the six sources was cited:

1. Jenifer Cruikshank, (2 full quotes, 1 paraphrase)
2. Dan Gleason, (1 full quote, 1 partial quote, 6 paraphrases)

3. Rick Boatner, (4 partial quotes, 2 paraphrases)
4. Barbara Gleason, (3 paraphrases)
5. Devon Ashbridge, (1 full quote, 1 paraphrase)
6. Angie Marzano, (1 full quote, 1 partial quote, 1 paraphrase)

It's also a good idea to examine articles for balance. Consider gender, ethnicity, age, disability, politics, religion, or any other kind of difference that may relate to the issue.

The "Starlings" article, for example, quotes four women and two men. The male sources get six combined quotes, and the female sources get five, which shows gender equity for a science-related topic.

What About Quoting Extreme Opinions or Mistruths?

Journalists, young and old, have a responsibility to share the truth. They also must carefully weigh when or if to include extreme opinions, determining whether to effectively censor sources if they do not serve the public interest. (Thankfully, your students are not breaking news with their articles, which is where many false claims, rumors, and mistruths take root.)

Of course, sources who speak mistruths should not be quoted or paraphrased, period. But what happens if a source spouts off opinions that are offensive or even abhorrent? Students should always consider the public good when making decisions about whom to quote, and they should avoid sensationalism.

A quick review of the SPJ's (2014) Code of Ethics can be enlightening. It states, journalists should:

Support the open and civil exchange of views, even views they find repugnant.

However, there is also this counterweight:

Balance the public's need for information against potential harm or discomfort.

Professional journalists usually discuss with their editors and colleagues what to do with a source who states facts or opinions in an offensive manner. They debate potential harm or discomfort against the public's need to know what others think.

Your students have an obligation to talk with each other and to you if they face similar situations. Coach them to ask: *Who does this quote serve? Is it helpful or harmful to understanding this issue? Is it necessary to understand this issue?*

Writing a Journalistic Closing

Closing paragraphs are robust and efficient, often providing one last great quote from a source that helps transition the article away from all the problems and toward solutions. The closing is a good place to focus on the future and to identify practical, action-oriented next steps.

A scaffold for students to use to craft powerful endings might look like this:

- Describe what can be done in the future to make the issue better.
- Add a quote from one or more sources with details or opinions about solutions.
- Describe (and link to) ways for readers to get assistance or contribute to solutions.

In Figure 7.3, you'll notice how the "Starlings" article follows this structure.

The best closings satisfy the reader's intrinsic desire to make sense of a complex problem and to feel some degree of agency over it. Students can and should make it easy for their readers to act.

FIGURE 7.3   **Show students a strong closing from a mentor text to help them see how to effectively wrap up their articles with solution-oriented information.**

Closing Structure

Describe what can be done to make the issue better in the future.

"People who live in a house in Eugene can put any food waste they do generate into their yard debris container," she said, and those who live in apartments could try reaching out to a neighbor or a participating restaurant nearby.

"It doesn't take a lot of effort," Marzano added, but has many benefits.

Add a quote from a source who gives more details or an opinion about solutions.

"In the case of bird feeders, it's a little easier to deter starlings," Barbara Gleason said. She recommends people use a suet feeder and put it in a cage so the starlings can't reach in.

There are "all sorts of bird feeder designs" that can discourage starlings, Boatner said.

Describe how readers can get assistance or can offer to help.

Farmers, landfill operators, and others dealing with large populations can contact a wildlife control agent with the U.S. Department of Agriculture. There's an office of the department's wildlife services program in Portland.

Excerpted from the article "Starlings in Oregon are an invasive pest to some, a fascinating species facing 'bio bigotry' to others," by Megan Banta, *The Eugene Register-Guard*

Credit: The Journalistic Learning Initiative

At the same time, no one expects journalists (or students) to solve complicated, nuanced issues by the end of one article, so students do not need to feel compelled to fix anything by the closing. They should aim for their audience to understand the problem and any potential solutions better than they did before reading.

Introducing Students to Associated Press Style

It's common for organizations to have style guides with rules for how written communication should be expressed and formatted. Companies and institutions create internal style books to promote clear, coordinated, front-facing communication for clients and customers. Examples include Ben & Jerry's, BuzzFeed, NASA, the National Park Service, and the City of New York.

Before students finish their drafts and move into feedback and revision stages, you might have them apply a few style rules from *The Associated Press Stylebook* (the *AP Stylebook*). Published continuously since 1953, the *AP Stylebook* contains hundreds of rules for word usage, grammar, and punctuation that guide journalists, editors, and communications experts to write efficiently. Because language is constantly evolving, the guidebook is updated every other year with new words. For example, in 2019 journalists were given instruction about how to use the words "deepfake" and "cryptocurrency" (Associated Press, 2019).

Table 7.1 shows five of the most applicable AP style rules to teach students.

TABLE 7.1 Five Style Rules from the Associated Press

AP STYLE RULES		
	Rules	**Examples**
Numbers	Spell out one-digit numbers.	one, two, three . . .
	Use numerals for two-digit numbers (10 and above).	10, 21, 185 . . .
	Ages and percentages are always numerals.	4 years old, 51% . . .
	Try not to begin a sentence with a number, because if you do, you *must* spell it out.	Six hundred and fifty-nine students stepped onto . . .

continues

	Rules	Examples
Time	If it's the exact hour, don't include :00. Use a.m. and p.m. for time, not AM and PM or am and pm	It started at 9 a.m.
Days of Week	Spell out days of week (no abbreviations). You don't need both a day of the week *and* a date. (If it's within one week of publication, use the day. If longer than a week, use the date.)	Every Wednesday and Friday, the center opens to students. It's happening on June 11.
Said	A source's name goes in front of *said,* not after. Use *said* (not *exclaimed, whispered,* etc.) to avoid introducing unnecessary tone and potential bias.	"I can't believe it," Ramirez said.
Verb Tenses	Events are told in the past tense. Issues are usually described in the present tense. Source attribution is *always in the past* tense (because your conversation was in the past), so use "said" not "says."	The food fight *left* the cafeteria a mess. Food fights *are* more of a problem this year than last. Even though starlings like the dump, they are not welcome, she *said.*

Ready for Critique?

Before they turn their writing over to peer readers for notes and revision tips, students should have an organized rough draft that includes a lede, quotes and paraphrasing from sources, quantitative and qualitative details, and a closing. Their paragraphs should be numerous and skinny, each just a sentence or two in length.

We recommend that reporting teams read their drafts aloud to listen for grammatical errors, which are often easier heard than seen. We also recommend that writers use spelling and grammar tools, as many professional writers do. This allows their peer readers to focus on more complex tasks such as identifying information gaps and noting unclear language or unnecessary repetition, which we will outline in the next chapter.

CHAPTER 8

Revising Their Story

"In order for students to be open to giving and receiving critique, I think they need to see learning and writing as something that is fluid and evolving and not finite."

—Middle School English Teacher

WRITING EXCELS WHEN IT BECOMES a team sport. Because we are often too close to our own work, even the most celebrated writers have editors; a second set of eyes can offer constructive feedback and elevate writing to higher levels.

Societal pressure to please or be perfect, however, leads many young writers to falsely assume their initial efforts should be flawless. Such a perspective can constrict expression. Helping students understand that effective writing is a multidraft process can free them.

The penultimate stage of journalistic learning is to have students connect with peer readers to get meaningful feedback on their first drafts. This is where school mirrors the world of work, which is becoming ever more specialized and collaborative.

What today is called knowledge work often requires teams of people with diverse skills to asynchronously create complex services or products. For example, software developers regularly may work with writers and editors, who may collaborate separately with artists, musicians, or filmmakers, who may connect with project managers, sales teams, and legal departments. Drafts of writing or other creative work often pass through many sets of eyes and receive constructive feedback at every stage.

Establishing a Culture of Critique

Good critique doesn't just happen in a language arts classroom. The skill must be taught and practiced ahead of time. Many teachers work hard to build a culture of critique in which intrinsically motivated student writers feel they can be vulnerable with their work and open to peer criticism. Students exhibit a kind of relaxed courage, freely soliciting advice from peers or stating what they think of a work in progress, despite social hierarchies that also exist outside the classroom.

Building this type of culture begins early in the school year, often with identifying and then consistently following norms that honor the processes of learning rather than the products of learning (or the byproducts, for example, grades and credits).

What does it look like in practice to embrace all the ways that learning sputters, falters, and feels frustrating? You might choose to adopt a slogan for your classroom that signals a philosophy of continual improvement and post it somewhere for all students to see. Working under a hand-drawn sign that states, "This class operates in permanent beta mode," for example, is a reminder of the heart of progress: trial and error. Or you might use the Marines-motto-turned-Bear-Grylls-meme, "Improvise. Adapt. Overcome." Whatever slogan you choose, establish an ethos of experimentation and improvisation and infuse it into everything that happens in the room. This implies permission for you and your students to be transparent with errors, misunderstandings, and missteps. It helps novice writers understand the value of their own growth as it emerges, not just at the end.

Another practice is to look for ways to frame learning and work as collaborative rather than competitive. In this way, students begin to see each other as resources and to view their community as one of abundance versus scarcity. Collaborators bond and support one another in a way that competitors just can't.

For example, if you have a student who is great with identifying colorful quotes or one who seems able to knock out effective ledes without too much trouble, ask them if they wouldn't mind being a resource for others. If they agree, send reporting teams over to them for assistance. You don't have to be the only source of insight and support.

Professional and scholastic journalists have the best of both worlds: they often work in close-knit newsrooms that share a common purpose, and they regularly compete with other publications to be the best at what they do. Their learning processes can be messy and collaborative and critical, even as they strive for finished products that are refined and singular. The experience of working in a local newsroom is a powerful one, and if you can structure your classroom in this way, it can be quite motivating.

Even in the most supportive environment, however, young writers may be hesitant to speak candidly about the work of their peers. They can be shy about reading a friend's draft and saying, "This doesn't make sense." They may fear they will offend. Or they may think they are the ones with a comprehension problem, just not smart enough to get what the writer is doing. Helping them to see honest feedback as an asset is essential.

One strategy that can help depersonalize the feedback process is to teach students in advance to say hard truths in a straightforward and specific way, without apology or the expectation of conflict. Sentence frames can be useful:

- "This is an important point, but _____ makes it harder to understand."
- "I think what you are trying to say is _____, but it's coming across as _____."
- "One question I have here is _____."

Clear expectations and a manageable set of well-defined proofreading tasks are critical to efficient peer editing. Our readers' workshop model is designed to take place over a couple of class sessions and to produce specific evidence for revision in three ways:

1. Identifying information gaps
2. Noting unnecessary repetition
3. Suggesting where to divide long paragraphs

We do not ask students to focus on correcting grammar, spelling, or style. As noted in the last chapter, these are more efficiently handled prior to a reader's workshop using automated no-cost spelling and grammar software.

Likewise, we do not ask peers to focus on organization problems due to the complexity of the feedback that would be needed to produce clear action steps for young writers. If there is a simple suggestion, such as moving a couple paragraphs around, editors should feel free to point it out, of course. We also recommend that you meet with students prior to peer editing to read their work and make organizational suggestions.

Organizing a Readers' Workshop

The entire class will benefit from collaborating with new peers at this stage of the project. To date, students have been working in reporting teams of three to four students. Once they have a draft article, they need readers with fresh

FIGURE 8.1   **Prior to editing and publishing, reporting teams move into new publishing teams.**

Reporting and Publishing Teams

ISSUE A	First, make reporting teams of 3–4 students	ISSUE H
ISSUE B		ISSUE I
ISSUE C		ISSUE J
ISSUE D		ISSUE K
ISSUE E	ISSUE F	ISSUE G

Later, regroup students into several publishing teams

ISSUE A	ISSUE G
ISSUE B	ISSUE H
ISSUE C	ISSUE I
ISSUE D	ISSUE J
ISSUE E	ISSUE K
ISSUE F	

ISSUE A	ISSUE G
ISSUE B	ISSUE H
ISSUE C	ISSUE I
ISSUE D	ISSUE J
ISSUE E	ISSUE K
ISSUE F	

ISSUE A	ISSUE G
ISSUE B	ISSUE H
ISSUE C	ISSUE I
ISSUE D	ISSUE J
ISSUE E	ISSUE K
ISSUE F	

Credit: The Journalistic Learning Initiative

eyes and energy, specifically readers who do not know as much about the issue they've been pursuing for weeks.

This is the time to create publishing teams ("pub teams"). The new groups serve as first readers on draft articles and will work together later to design an online newspaper.

You may recall Figure 3.2 from Chapter 3, which shows how pub teams might be organized in a class of 33 to 34 students. For a refresher, see Figure 8.1, which shows 11 reporting teams regrouped into three pub teams.

Once students have gathered into publication teams, they should pair up and exchange draft articles for a first read. We encourage writers to bring their entire article to the workshop, rather than just a third of it, so that peer editors can offer suggestions on all of it.

You will need to decide in advance whether drafts should be read on paper or digitally. There are pros and cons to each choice. Printing out drafts can be an expensive luxury in some classrooms or burdensome if there is limited, restricted, or inconvenient printer access. However, paper is tangible and allows students to efficiently mark suggestions with a pencil or highlighter and avoid electronic distractions. Some readers also have an easier time spotting mistakes on paper. On the other hand, reading digital drafts can allow for fluid and asynchronous two-way communication and is the way most professional editing is done today.

In our media-saturated world, we are exposed to well-written stories from which we passively learn syntax and style. Consequently, having students read their own work to a partner aloud can lead them to hear and self-correct awkward phrasing or questionable passages themselves.

However, we believe that all writers must retain the agency to accept or reject suggestions. It's important to explain to peer editors that they are *suggesting* changes, not *making* changes to a draft. If they are working digitally, ask them to use comments or to use a suggestion-only mode, not an edit mode.

The duties of first readers (peer editors) are clear cut:

- Read the entire draft first, without marking, to understand the big picture and learn about the issue.
- Read the draft a second time to mark suggestions.

The specific tasks of peer editors can be anything you want them to focus on. We suggest three areas:

1. Ask questions about the issue to identify information gaps.
2. Note instances of unnecessary repetition to be more concise.
3. Note instances where long blocks of text can be divided to improve readability.

We encourage you to guide the class ahead of time in how to make suggestions in these three areas. Give them time to practice so they build familiarity and competence before moving to work on a peer's writing.

A simple one- or two-paragraph hypothetical student draft that is imperfect can be quite illustrative. For example:

William Baxter is the Chaplain, Reverend of the United Campus Ministry. Baxter had gotten involved with the university food pantry when he became the chaplain for the United Campus Ministry a little over 4 years ago. The food pantry had been going for about a year when he got involved. Baxter is the manager of the food pantry, his job other than being a Chaplain is getting food for the pantry by going to Food for This

County once a week to pick up food and taking it back to the pantry to organize the food.

Ask students to identify and write in the margins a couple of questions they wonder about. They can go through each of the 5 W's and H and also think of a quantitative question.

For example, in the paragraph above:

- *Where is the food pantry located (address)?*
- *How much food does Baxter pick up each week on average?*

Next, students can circle or highlight unnecessary repetition. Our rule of thumb is to try not to repeat a word in a paragraph more than twice. For example, in the above draft we see that:

- Baxter's name is repeated *three times*
- The name of the ministry is repeated *twice*
- "Food" is repeated *six times*
- "Pantry" is repeated *five times*

Finally, ask students to mark where the writer might divide this long paragraph into shorter ones. (Either in the middle of the four sentences or before the last sentence in the example above.)

Remind students that they are not fixing the issues, just noting them. They should read carefully and thoughtfully with an eye toward helping writers see their blind spots.

Timing will be a challenge during the readers' workshop, as it often is in the English classroom, because neither the drafts nor the student readers are standardized. Some students will receive longer articles to review than others. Some students are quicker readers and take to editing naturally and easily, while others may work more slowly. Some drafts will need more suggestions.

Plan what you can have students do if they finish while others are still working. For instance, you might have them switch drafts with other waiting students so articles get multiple reads. Or, they could begin to identify photos that will accompany their published articles.

Following Up With a Writers' Workshop

Once drafts have been marked up, allow individual writers to read and absorb the feedback in private. Reporting teams then should reconvene to compare and discuss what they've received.

Because writing clearly, credibly, and concisely is one of the more complex and difficult academic skills, and mastery of the craft takes time and patience, students may get discouraged seeing the revision notes. That's okay. Many writers are a bit touchy when it comes to criticism, even over mild suggestions.

Novice writers who rarely receive enough feedback during the writing process, or who don't get a chance to revise their work, may feel especially concerned. The one-and-done writing practices that prepare students for standardized testing leaves them with little natural resilience for criticism.

A guided revision process can help students to slow down and thoughtfully consider suggestions. You can call this next stage a writers' workshop and present students with clear expectations:

1. Read feedback with an open mind.
2. Ask your peer reviewer questions if you don't understand their comments.
3. Discuss suggestions with your cowriters to see if you all agree.
4. Think of your article as a service to your future readers.

Hardest for young writers to fix will be the requests for more information. Filling in gaps that they didn't realize existed usually requires more research, reading, and writing. It's much more labor-intensive compared to the other revision tasks they may face. Encourage students to address information gaps first, even if they need to email sources again or do more online reading.

Student writers should not just automatically start researching and answering every question posed by a first reader. Some of the questions may be irrelevant, and others may lead to overcomplicating a story. Writers need to discuss together why they think a question is being asked. They should determine for themselves if more information would add to or distract from their story.

The simple decision-making scaffold shown in Table 8.1 can be helpful for student writers to analyze reader feedback.

TABLE 8.1   **Decision-Making Scaffold for Evaluating Reader Feedback**

WRITERS' CONVERSATION: SHOULD WE ADD REQUESTED INFORMATION?	
No, because:	**Yes. Now what?**
The information is already here. *The reader just didn't read carefully.*	Is the information already in our notes? *Find it and add.*
The information is already here. *However, we need to make it clearer.*	Can we do an online search for this information? *Who will take responsibility for this question?*
The information they are requesting is *not relevant to understanding this issue.*	Can we contact one of our sources to ask them? *Who will take responsibility for asking them?*

A bit easier for students is the task of eliminating unnecessary repetition and breaking long paragraphs into breezier ones. Before they start revising, however, show a model and let them practice editing practice on a common paragraph such as the example in Figure 8.2.

FIGURE 8.2   **Dividing long paragraphs and eliminating unnecessary repetition can lower word count in journalistic writing, making for a breezier read.**

Evidence That Revision Works

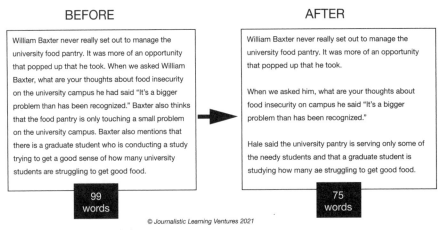

BEFORE

William Baxter never really set out to manage the university food pantry. It was more of an opportunity that popped up that he took. When we asked William Baxter, what are your thoughts about food insecurity on the university campus he had said "It's a bigger problem than has been recognized." Baxter also thinks that the food pantry is only touching a small problem on the university campus. Baxter also mentions that there is a graduate student who is conducting a study trying to get a good sense of how many university students are struggling to get good food.

99 words

AFTER

William Baxter never really set out to manage the university food pantry. It was more of an opportunity that popped up that he took.

When we asked him, what are your thoughts about food insecurity on campus he said "It's a bigger problem than has been recognized."

Hale said the university pantry is serving only some of the needy students and that a graduate student is studying how many ae struggling to get good food.

75 words

© Journalistic Learning Ventures 2021

Credit: The Journalistic Learning Initiative

Helping Writers Self-Assess

As part of their revision process, you might want to have your students assess their own drafts to identify other gaps or mistakes. A simple handout that matches the criteria you have established can help writers keep track of all the components.

Consider asking them to assess their own:

- Organization of ideas
- Specific word choice
- Quantitative details
- Qualitative details
- Repeated words
- Use of quotes
- Punctuation
- Spelling

See Table A.3 in Appendix A for an example of a student self-assessment.

Giving Writers Formative Feedback

We encourage you to meet with reporting teams before they move into the publication stage of the project. You might require students to keep multiple drafts of their writing in order to document how the article has changed over time. This kind of self-reflective discussion helps students see their own growth as learners and can be quietly powerful for them.

You might also choose to collect and read their drafts in order to offer them additional notes and get a clear sense of exactly what they would plan to publish. This allows you to head off problems such as accidental bias or insufficient attribution of source material. A formative assessment tool that aligns with the criteria on a student self-assessment handout may be useful. See Table A.4 in Appendix A for an example.

Choosing a Competency-Based Grading Philosophy

Writers in professional newsrooms rarely experience complete project failure. If their work does not pass muster the first time they submit it to an editor, they get more chances to improve it. If they run into roadblocks, they ask for and receive help. Writers simply rework their articles over and over until they meet the high bar for publication. They are given deadline extensions all the time because of how uncertain the process is, and rarely is a feature story ever permanently canned because it failed. (Nor is a staff writer's pay docked for needing extra time on an article.)

You might consider adapting this philosophy as you consider how to grade the project. If publication is the bar, then all articles must meet it for a grade. Perhaps students who miss the mark and need more time to revise their writing can be given an incomplete until they produce a publishable article, at which point they receive an "A" for clearing the bar. Many scholastic journalism classes in high school run on this "A or Incomplete" competency-based grading philosophy, and it may work for your language arts classroom, too.

In the next chapter, we will discuss more ways to assess and measure student growth, including looking at the College and Career Readiness Standards for English Language Arts. Now the final stage of the journalistic learning project is upon us: allowing writer-researchers to transition into designer-publishers in order to release their hard-won stories into the wild.

Journalistic Skills for Every Career: Documentary Filmmaker

A surprising number of endeavors begin with written proposals. While oral and visually dynamic pitch meetings play a critical role in connecting people around new ideas, written proposals and reports are also foundational. They serve as permanent records of hopes, dreams, objectives, and goals and especially of iterative progress. Documentary filmmakers receive and evaluate feedback at the proposal stage and get accustomed to working in collaborative, critique-oriented environments. Working under pressure of deadlines to review and edit writing drafts can be an exhilarating and highly rewarding path to the finished film.

CHAPTER 9

Sharing Their Story

"I felt like all the different steps really helped me write the article pretty fluently."

—11th-Grader

JOURNALISM IS MEANT TO BE SHARED. The type of news writing we've outlined in this book is not an intimate one such as found in a letter or a private journal or even a work of fiction, where it may feel that the author is sharing secrets directly and personally with you the reader. Journalistic writing exists to spread far and wide, to make the complex understandable for mass audiences, and to spread truth like a tonic among the uninformed.

From a journalist's initial questions to all of the research, interviews, writing, and revision, publication is what motivates the process. Even though we've reserved discussion of why and how to publish your students' work for this final chapter, publication is not merely a byproduct of the learning that came before—it's the goal.

For language arts teachers who do not also teach a journalism elective or advise student media, it may be tempting to see publication as an unnecessary activity. *Doesn't this take even more class time away from literature, poetry, and other worthy studies? Students are used to writing for a grade, so what more motivation do they really need?*

A strong case can be made for English teachers to cap off their journalistic learning project by guiding students to create digital websites to serve as public vehicles for their stories. In this chapter, we present the rationale for online publication in the language arts classroom, as well as some considerations to think through in advance. We also address reasons and ways students can use responsible social media practices to spread the word about their work. We offer an alternative to digital publication and present ideas for honoring and celebrating student accomplishments at the end of a rigorous, challenging unit. Finally, we provide ideas for measuring new skills and understanding through summative assessment and feedback.

Moving Stories Online

It's not difficult today to create a website, and your students may even already have experience doing so. Because they have grown up with a fast-expanding, easily accessible, and relatively cheap internet, however, they may not appreciate just how much agency they have compared to earlier generations. Student voices today have greater reach than at any time in history.

We encourage you to help your students understand their relative privilege within a historic perspective. You might point out that during the print era, basically the 1980s and before, student voices were limited to their own school print publications. In many cases, school newspapers and magazines were either approved or censored by adults; teachers, principals and even superintendents could spike a story, relegating student work to the trash can.

This continues in some schools today, since students' press rights vary by state. True, in the past students who wanted to protest or call attention to an issue in their community could submit letters to the editor in local newspapers or magazines, but these could be edited or dismissed out of hand for any number of reasons, including space, tone, or content. The expressed concerns of young people have often been minimized, simplified, or simply unsought and unacknowledged by journalism's gatekeepers.

In the 1990s, internet subscribers got space online to make personal webpages, allowing them to publish without the approval of anyone. By the early 2000s, personal websites proliferated, but they were typically read-only experiences, with no possibility of interaction. They also weren't easy to find or share. This type of internet experience is known as Web 1.0.

Around 2005, digital technology progressed, giving rise to a more participatory and interactive online experience with opportunities for shopping, blogging, news consumption, photo-sharing, and, of course, social media. This Web 2.0 was an explosion of digital commerce, opinion, information, and multimedia. Free and low-cost website design tools and hosting platforms expanded the reach of anyone who took the time to learn how to publish online.

By 2022, there were nearly 1.17 billion websites on the internet, with three new sites created every second (Huss, 2022). Of those, according to Huss, only 17% of the sites are considered active, meaning they are updated with some frequency. Voices from outside the journalism establishment are free to be published, and stories that would not have found a platform 30 years ago can now be read. The world of ideas, facts, truth, and perspective is more dynamic, flexible, equitable, and complicated because of it.

In acknowledgement of this two-decade sea change, education standards in many states have been updated to reflect an expectation that secondary students use modern publication tools in school. For example, 41 states plus the District of Columbia and 4 territories have adopted the Common Core Career and College Readiness Standards for English Language Arts (CCR) as of 2022.

One of the CCR anchor standards for writing states: "Use technology, including the Internet, to produce and publish writing and to interact and collaborate with others" (CCSS.ELA-LITERACY.CCRA.W.6). Luckily, the technology to do this is likely already at your students' fingertips.

Balancing Online Access and Privacy

There are several ways for students to publish their articles online. You could make a class website and give each reporting team a page to display their article. You could have students each make their own independent webpage using a free online service and then link all the pages to a common classroom website. Or you could allow the existing publication teams the opportunity to organize their own public-facing online news sites.

This third option allows your students to take responsibility for the creation of a novel product and to practice working collaboratively. The energy in the room shifts from the individual detail work of rewriting and editing to joint ideation and sensemaking. Publishing teams will experience a sense of agency in coming up with a name and design for their news site.

There's also the thrill of publishing and realizing one's work will reach an authentic audience. Consider that nearly all other school assignments meet one set of eyes—the teacher's. We find that when students realize that their peers, parents, and community will view their work, their level of commitment and ownership increases significantly, as does their sense of responsibility to their publication teammates.

Students realize their interview subjects and sources have entrusted them to ethically convey their story, and so greater attention is placed on accuracy and getting things right. The rush of working on deadline adds excitement to the end of the project.

There are privacy considerations to think through in advance of online publication. You may need to check the rules of your school or district to see if they limit what your students are allowed to share online. The age of your students is also a factor. Middle school and high school teachers may have different concerns, including:

- Should students use their full names on their bylines, or just a first name?
- Should the website be shared in a limited way, or be open to the public?

We believe communities need more well-researched articles about the concerns of young people, so we encourage teachers to let their students' final pieces out into the larger world with as much transparency and reach as possible.

We also encourage teachers to share their students' work (with appropriate consent) with local news outlets for republication. The excitement of seeing one's words and byline reach a broader community is empowering, especially when the subject matter articulates a perspective that has the potential to influence public opinion.

Publication also allows for sources to read and even respond to students' writing. Publication allows your students to add their articles to future writing portfolios, either for academic or employment purposes. Publication brings your students' writing into the arena of ideas and may even contribute to the common good.

Providing Checklists for Publication

Consider structuring this final stage of the project in a way that gives your students autonomy while holding them responsible for some of the professional journalistic practices for published articles. You can do this by having each publishing team select two members to be coeditors-in-chief. These student leaders can help organize and encourage their teams and oversee a few details that need to come together to create cohesive publications in a short amount of time.

Give class editors a checklist to ensure their website's homepage includes:

- Title of the news outlet
- School name
- City name
- Date of publication

- Headlines
- Fair-use photographs
- Links to articles
- A single simple, consistent font (for example, Lato, Arial, Verdana)
- Type size that is large and consistent across all articles (14 pt. is good for readability across various screens)

After editors create the website, they can give access to each member of the publication team so they can upload their articles. If you have organized the publication teams as described in Chapter 7, your class will have several publications, each with 10 to 12 articles. While the publications will look different and have different names, the articles will be the same across the three sites. Although it may seem redundant, multiple websites allow each student to gain experience with writing headlines, choosing a fair-use photograph to illustrate a complex topic, and being an active participant of a publication team.

Formatting Articles for Publication

Team members should be responsible for adhering to three basic news structures for publication:

1. Writing headlines
2. Adding author bylines
3. Choosing a fair-use photograph and giving appropriate credit

Teach students to keep their headlines short, from 10 to 15 words maximum. The headlines should be accurate and specific, written in the present tense, with keywords that describe the article's topic or main point. The strongest headlines include a geographical location to indicate that the reporters have tackled the issue from a local or regional angle.

Here are some headlines written by the high school students in our journalistic learning program in 2022:

- Title IX: 50 Years and Counting
- Portland's Housing Supply Problem: Will the Shortage Have a Solution?
- The Intersection of Roe v. Wade and Adoptions in Oregon
- Wolves: A Nuisance to Some, a Magnificent Creature to Others

Bylines should be placed under the headline and above the text of the article so that readers can see who is responsible for the article prior to reading. Each student who contributed to the writing or research should be listed. Reporting teams might agree to organize multiple bylines alphabetically or in some other order.

Photographs and other images such as drawings or graphs attract reader attention and help to visually represent complex issues. Some students may wish to take their own photographs or create their own art, which is great and always preferable to borrowing images.

However, if time is short, the most efficient legal way to obtain free, high-quality photographs is to search for images licensed under Creative Commons. An international nonprofit organization, Creative Commons provides licenses for creators to use to offer their work to the public for fair use. These licenses allow anyone to download and republish the work under certain conditions, such as not modifying the photograph or not using it as part of a for-profit venture.

You don't need to go into the minutiae of copyright law, but take a moment to discuss the doctrine of fair use, so that students know that part of being a responsible digital creator or publisher means only using images with permission. Once students have selected a photograph and uploaded it to their article, they should give credit to the photographer either in a line of text below the photograph or at the bottom of the article.

What About Publishing Articles That Aren't Ready?

While publishing every student article is ideal, it may not be appropriate. The bar for publication should be set quite high so that it respects the sources who gave their time and so that the larger community of readers are presented with a publication that meets journalism standards for accuracy and fairness.

You can ask student editors to weigh the merits of each article under consideration. Do they believe it meets the standards that you have provided students in advance? If not, and time has run out for improvements, spiking or delaying the story's publication is recommended.

Using Social Media for Promotion

Social media can be a force for good, with young people using their platforms to drive positive change. For example, Sedona Price was a member of the

University of Oregon women's basketball team in 2021 when she used TikTok and Twitter to call out unequal workout facilities for female and male athletes at the NCAA March Madness basketball tournament (Mickanen, 2021). Her videos started a national dialogue leading to consideration and improvements.

Businesses, government agencies, and nonprofits use social media to share information and connect with people every day. Some organizations have dedicated social media managers who create content and interact with people across multiple platforms. Realtors, educators, doctors, entertainers, artists, and contractors, as well as local, state, and federal agencies, such as first responders, elected officials, and public safety workers increasingly use social media to further their work.

Student publications have little chance of making an impact, or even being read, without online promotion. Ideas for instructors to consider:

- Create new social media accounts for your classroom and share out links to student articles. Students and parents can follow and then repost or share from their own accounts. The upside is you (or your editors) control the account. The downside is that building a base of new followers will be slow.
- Let students use their own social media accounts to spread the word. A benefit to this approach is that students probably already have followers. A concern is that some students won't have social media and others may understandably resist blurring the boundary between school and personal interests.
- Ask school or district accounts to share links to student work. Many schools have active social media accounts. You might check to see if whoever runs your account would be willing to share out the links to publications or individual stories.

Since social media is constantly evolving, it's difficult for adults to give relevant advice to students about creating social media content that will be of interest to their peers, so we recommend that you turn over the task of promotion to them. Ask students to consider their potential readers. How can they share their articles in different ways with:

- Peers
- Relatives

- Other teachers
- Their sources
- Academics in the field
- Relevant businesses or services
- Government or elected officials
- Nonprofits in the field
- Professional journalists who cover the topic

Encourage students to get creative on social media without compromising a professional tone that matches the seriousness of their topic. Good judgment is always necessary, and young people may need to be reminded that while social media feels ephemeral, it's not. There are tools that allow people to see past versions of websites, even if they were edited or deleted. Youthful opinions online can have a long life and disrupt careers years later.

This doesn't mean students should not share what they believe in; it means they should be thoughtful and intentional about anything they post online.

Journalistic Skills for Every Career: Social Media Manager

Social media managers produce editorial content and connect with audiences across diverse social platforms in order to promote and represent their organization. A typical day might include creating, scheduling, and publishing unique posts on Instagram, TikTok, LinkedIn, Facebook, and other social channels to engage followers and build new audiences. Social media managers work closely with members of their organization and outside collaborators to strategically promote their brand with upcoming announcements, events, or new products. They create a cohesive online tone and presence for the brand, while tracking engagement and responding to messages. Social media professionals work to build brand recognition and trust.

Making Corrections to Fix Mistakes

Correcting mistakes is an ethical obligation for journalists. It's often said that journalism is history's first draft, so the facts matter not just today but for future generations. Because errors are made at all levels of journalism—journalists are people, after all—every professional news outlet has a system for making corrections after publication. For example, *The New York Times* publishes and tracks corrections on a webpage that you can show your students: https://www.nytimes.com/section/corrections.

Teach students in advance of publication how they will be expected to correct errors. (A 5-minute mini lesson on this can also motivate students to check their facts one more time.) The correction process for students is simple:

1. Edit the online article to make it accurate.
2. Place a note at the bottom of the article in italics: *An earlier version of this article misstated* _____. *It was actually* _____.
3. Communicate with the person who pointed out the mistake to apologize for the error and thank them for pointing it out. Share the link to the corrected article with them.

An Alternative to Online Publication

Online publication is not for everyone, and sometimes good old-fashioned paper is the way to go for sharing student work. Interior hallways and common areas can be lined with student articles, using poster board and easels or placed directly on the walls.

Collections of students' printed articles can also be featured in the school media center, library, or office. Some teachers invite other classes to read and offer comments, reviews, or feedback on the displays. Public exhibits are meaningful for families and community members to see at school open house events.

Publication Day: A Time for Sharing, Reflecting, and Celebrating

Setting aside a class period for publication day celebration and reflection allows you and your students to spend time sharing, showcasing, and honoring weeks of work and learning. Your students have come a long way from their very first questions to their published articles. They stepped into the unknown, took risks, overcame frustrations, and probably vanquished some nerves along the way. Their articles are out in the world.

You might wish to set some time aside for students to independently read each of the articles produced in class. This could take the form of a gallery tour, asking students to move systematically around the room to different desks where laptops display the articles. Or it could be an in-class voting system in which students read articles and nominate them for various awards such as "Most Professional" or "Readers' Choice."

You might also provide time for writers to briefly present their project. Some teachers ask students to summarize their article for the class and share how they got past a roadblock or what they are most proud of. Mini presentations provide closure and create a positive narrative around what may have been a stressful time during research, interviewing, or writing.

This is also a great time to revisit any baseline writing or surveys students completed prior to the project's launch to see if their understanding about the news has changed. Ask students to add to their initial understanding so that they can see their growth:

- The news is . . .
- What are some ways journalists avoid bias (one-sidedness) in their work?
- What are examples of quantitative details (numbers) you might find in a news article?
- What are examples of qualitative details (description)you might find in a news article?
- What is important to remember when interviewing someone for a news story?
- Describe your confidence level as an online researcher and writer.

Finally, pizza, donuts, or a potluck with some free time to unwind may be in order. Celebrate the accomplishments of the class and the birth of their new publications. If you plan to teach this unit each year, a fun food-oriented tradition can distinguish both the project and your class culture, while making memories and creating a buzz that gives younger students something to anticipate.

Evaluating Student Learning

A project of this length and complexity can be measured in different ways. In earlier chapters, we've provided examples of formative assessments that you might use during various stages of learning. Here are some ideas for postproject summative assessments:

How to Measure Group Collaboration

You might consider having students evaluate their group effectiveness using a rubric that asks them to reflect on the levels of collaboration, participation, and commitment by each member of the team. Students can note attendance issues that may have led to some members not contributing as much as expected. Each student can determine what percent of the article they contributed. (A sample student evaluation handout is provided as Table A.5 in Appendix A.)

How to Measure Writing Skills

If you desire a way to gauge students individually, you might consider having students take a summative writing assessment that requires them to watch and listen to an interview on video, read a transcript, or both, then write a short journalistic article. (A sample rubric for such an assessment is provided as Table A.6 in Appendix A.)

How to Measure Project Engagement and Value

Student feedback can be helpful for you to understand the strengths and weaknesses of the project and to improve it for next year. Consider asking students to measure their own understanding and skills retrospectively (before the project) and now. You can ask them about their understanding of the media, journalistic ethics, fact-checking, spotting bias, interviewing and more. (A sample student feedback form is offered as Figure A.2 in Appendix A.)

Any or all of these summative tools can be used to help you formulate grades or report standards-based competencies. If your school uses the Common Core English Language Arts Standards, you can find a checklist of anchor standards that we've aligned to each stage of the project as Table A.1 in Appendix A.

Growing a Project Into a Program

The purpose of this book is to support the inclusion of journalistic writing and research in English language arts classrooms. But we also know journalistic writing can become exciting and energizing for teachers and students who want to investigate, tell, and preserve their school's stories. The stories students produce can be exhilarating in their ambition and depth of research, not to mention effort. (See Appendix C for an exemplary student article.) We've seen teachers use the momentum of their multiweek project to spark a new journalism elective or club at their school the following year.

Starting a new journalism program, or restoring a moribund existing one from near death, takes a lot of work, but the payoff is a front row seat where you get to watch young people make hard decisions, support and guide each other, and grow as ethical communicators and leaders. If your school doesn't have a journalism program yet and this project sparks interest, we encourage you to go for it. Examples of highly respected organizations that support new scholastic journalism programs and teachers are listed as example A.9 in Appendix A.

Journalistic learning ignites students' curiosity, encourages freer self-expression, and nourishes their innate potential to learn. Educators report that it reinvigorates their enthusiasm for teaching as they guide students in exploration of topics that are timely, relevant, and therefore more meaningful.

We are committed to broader adoption of journalistic learning because we've witnessed firsthand the tremendous difference it can make in students' lives. Young people falsely labeled reluctant learners or who seem disengaged with school have exhibited profound shifts in their relationship to education and in their overall academic outcomes. Our approach acknowledges and honors students' intrinsic interests and encourages deeper explorations of student-generated topics.

Equally inspiring is watching students become civically engaged. They gain a new sense of connection to their community and its concerns and in their own ability to contribute to public conversations about those concerns.

One participating student said it best:

I was passionate about (the topic), and since I was passionate about it, I had energy behind it. So, I needed to crack the case, right? I needed to get these answers from these people. And once I had them, it was awesome. Because I had what I needed. And they were willing to do it. And it was just watching them tell their stories. Watching people be people is like the funnest thing in the world, because watching people explain their life's passion behind something . . . you can't make that in a lab, right? You can't create that. That's raw. And that's what's so fun [. . . .] Being passionate about it will cause your interviewee to be passionate about it and your passion [. . . they're] going to collide like particles, and it's going to explode, and the universe is gonna be there and boom! Like, there's your new universe.

We invite you to join the journalistic learning community and share how you're applying this book's principles and strategies in your classroom. Teachers interested in a deeper dive are invited to inquire about self-paced online professional development and ongoing support, as detailed on the Journalistic Learning Initiative website: https://journalisticlearning.org/.

APPENDIX A

Instructional Tools and Templates

Section A.1, Table A.1: Career and College Readiness Anchor Standards (Chapter 2)

The stages of a journalistic learning project align with the national English Language Arts College and Career Readiness Anchor Standards:

Standards Practiced
Reading: 9 out of 10
Writing: 8 out of 10
Speaking and Listening: 6 out of 6
Language: 6 out of 6

Total:
30 out of 32 standards (92%)

College & Career Readiness Anchor Standards
for English Language Arts (2010)

✓ = practiced   ✗ = not targeted

	COLLEGE & CAREER READINESS — READING		JL PROJECT STAGES
Key Ideas And Details			
✓	CCSS.ELA-LITERACY. CCRA.R.1	Read closely to determine what the text says explicitly and to make logical inferences from it; cite specific textual evidence when writing or speaking to support conclusions drawn from the text.	Research & Investigation
✓	CCSS.ELA-LITERACY. CCRA.R.2	Determine central ideas or themes of a text and analyze their development; summarize the key supporting details and ideas.	Research & Investigation
✓	CCSS.ELA-LITERACY. CCRA.R.3	Analyze how and why individuals, events, or ideas develop and interact over the course of a text.	Research & Investigation
Craft And Structure			
✓	CCSS.ELA-LITERACY. CCRA.R.4	Interpret words and phrases as they are used in a text, including determining technical, connotative, and figurative meanings, and analyze how specific word choices shape meaning or tone.	Research & Investigation, Peer Editing
✓	CCSS.ELA-LITERACY. CCRA.R.5	Analyze the structure of texts, including how specific sentences, paragraphs, and larger portions of the text (e.g., a section, chapter, scene, or stanza) relate to each other and the whole.	Research & Investigation, Peer Editing
✓	CCSS.ELA-LITERACY. CCRA.R.6	Assess how point of view or purpose shapes the content and style of a text.	Research & Investigation, Writing
Integration Of Knowledge And Ideas			
✓	CCSS.ELA-LITERACY. CCRA.R.7	Integrate and evaluate content presented in diverse media and formats, including visually and quantitatively, as well as in words.	Research & Investigation
✓	CCSS.ELA-LITERACY. CCRA.R.8	Delineate and evaluate the argument and specific claims in a text, including the validity of the reasoning as well as the relevance and sufficiency of the evidence.	Research & Investigation
✓	CCSS.ELA-LITERACY. CCRA.R.9	Analyze how two or more texts address similar themes or topics in order to build knowledge or to compare the approaches the authors take.	Research & Investigation
✓	CCSS.ELA-LITER-ACY.CCRA.R.10	Read and comprehend complex literary and informational texts independently and proficiently.	Research & Investigation

COLLEGE & CAREER READINESS — WRITING		JL PROJECT STAGES
Text Types And Purposes		
✗ CCSS.ELA-LITERACY. CCRA.W.1	Write arguments to support claims in an analysis of substantive topics or texts using valid reasoning and relevant and sufficient evidence.	N/A
✓ CCSS.ELA-LITERACY. CCRA.W.2	Write informative/explanatory texts to examine and convey complex ideas and information clearly and accurately through the effective selection, organization, and analysis of content.	Writing
✗ CCSS.ELA-LITERACY. CCRA.W.3	Write narratives to develop real or imagined experiences or events using effective technique, well-chosen details, and well-structured event sequences.	N/A
Production And Distribution Of Writing		
✓ CCSS.ELA-LITERACY. CCRA.W.4	Produce clear and coherent writing in which the development, organization, and style are appropriate to task, purpose, and audience.	Writing
✓ CCSS.ELA-LITERACY. CCRA.W.5	Develop and strengthen writing as needed by planning, revising, editing, rewriting, or trying a new approach.	Writing
✓ CCSS.ELA-LITERACY. CCRA.W.6	Use technology, including the Internet, to produce and publish writing and to interact and collaborate with others.	Publication, Promotion
Research To Build And Present Knowledge		
✓ CCSS.ELA-LITERACY. CCRA.W.7	Conduct short as well as more sustained research projects based on focused questions, demonstrating understanding of the subject under investigation.	Interviewing
✓ CCSS.ELA-LITERACY. CCRA. W.8	Gather relevant information from multiple print and digital sources, assess the credibility and accuracy of each source, and integrate the information while avoiding plagiarism.	Research & Investigation, Writing
✓ CCSS.ELA-LITERACY. CCRA.W.9	Draw evidence from literary or informational texts to support analysis, reflection, and research.	Research & Investigation, Writing
Range Of Writing		
✓ CCSS.ELA-LITERACY. CCRA.W.10	Write routinely over extended time frames (time for research, reflection, and revision) and shorter time frames (a single sitting or a day or two) for a range of tasks, purposes, and audiences.	Writing, Revision

COLLEGE & CAREER READINESS — SPEAKING AND LISTENING		JL PROJECT STAGES
Comprehension And Collaboration		
✓ CCSS.ELA-LITERACY. CCRA.SL.1	Prepare for and participate effectively in a range of conversations and collaborations with diverse partners, building on others' ideas and expressing their own clearly and persuasively.	Interviewing
✓ CCSS.ELA-LITERACY. CCRA.SL.1	Integrate and evaluate information presented in diverse media and formats, including visually, quantitatively, and orally.	Research & Investigation, Interviewing
✓ CCSS.ELA-LITERACY. CCRA.SL.1	Evaluate a speaker's point of view, reasoning, and use of evidence and rhetoric.	Interviewing
Presentation Of Knowledge And Ideas		
✓ CCSS.ELA-LITERACY. CCRA.SL.1	Present information, findings, and supporting evidence such that listeners can follow the line of reasoning and the organization, development, and style are appropriate to task, purpose, and audience.	Publication, Promotion
✓ CCSS.ELA-LITERACY. CCRA.SL.1	Make strategic use of digital media and visual displays of data to express information and enhance understanding of presentations.	Publication, Promotion
✓ CCSS.ELA-LITERACY. CCRA.SL.1	Adapt speech to a variety of contexts and communicative tasks, demonstrating command of formal English when indicated or appropriate.	Interviewing

COLLEGE & CAREER READINESS — LANGUAGE			JL PROJECT STAGES
Conventions Of Standard English			
✓	CCSS.ELA-LITERACY. CCRA.L.1	Demonstrate command of the conventions of standard English grammar and usage when writing or speaking.	Writing, Peer Editing
✓	CCSS.ELA-LITERACY. CCRA.L.1	Demonstrate command of the conventions of standard English capitalization, punctuation, and spelling when writing.	Writing, Peer Editing
Knowledge Of Language			
✓	CCSS.ELA-LITERACY. CCRA.L.1	Apply knowledge of language to understand how language functions in different contexts, to make effective choices for meaning or style, and to comprehend more fully when reading or listening.	Writing, Peer Editing
Vocabulary Acquisition And Use			
✓	CCSS.ELA-LITERACY. CCRA.L.1	Determine or clarify the meaning of unknown and multiple-meaning words and phrases by using context clues, analyzing meaningful word parts, and consulting general and specialized reference materials, as appropriate.	Research & Investigation, Writing, Peer Editing
✓	CCSS.ELA-LITERACY. CCRA.L.1	Demonstrate understanding of figurative language, word relationships, and nuances in word meanings.	Research & Investigation, Writing, Peer Editing
✓	CCSS.ELA-LITERACY. CCRA.L.1	Acquire and use accurately a range of general academic and domain-specific words and phrases sufficient for reading, writing, speaking, and listening at the college and career readiness level; demonstrate independence in gathering vocabulary knowledge when encountering an unknown term important to comprehension or expression.	Research & Investigation, Writing, Peer Editing

Section A.2, Figure A.1: Instructor Template: Request to Newspaper Editor or Publisher (Chapter 3)

This template can be used by educators to make an advance appeal to local newspapers for access to paywalled news articles.

Dear _____ :

   I'm a teacher/media specialist at _____ (school) in _____ (city). I'm writing to request your help in providing some of our students with complimentary online access to the _____ (title of newspaper).

   We are teaching a project that introduces students to their local news publications and has them experience the journalistic process of researching, interviewing, writing, and publishing on local topics that concern them.

   Our students need access to your publication to engage in the research portion of their investigative projects. They will learn how to effectively navigate and search the _____ (title of newspaper) for previous coverage and for potential community sources that they can interview. For many students, it will be the first time they have explored their local news. We believe this experience will give them valuable news literacy skills and engage them as future news readers and subscribers.

   Please support our students by providing free online access to use in class between now and _____ . You can reach me at _____ (phone/email).

   Warmly,

_____

Section A.3, Table A.2: Student Source Organizer (Chapter 5)

A source organizer can help students identify and organize potential sources during the research and pitch stage of the project.

Directions: Identify three potential sources you can interview about your issue:

Name		Job Title		
Email		Organization		
Circle Type of Source:	Academic	Service	Regulatory	
Circle Type of Questions:	Present	Past	Future	

Name		Job Title		
Email		Organization		
Circle Type of Source:	Academic	Service	Regulatory	
Circle Type of Questions:	Present	Past	Future	

Name		Job Title		
Email		Organization		
Circle Type of Source:	Academic	Service	Regulatory	
Circle Type of Questions:	Present	Past	Future	

Section A.4, Table A.3: Informative Writing Self-Assessment (Chapter 8)

Students can assess their writing during any stage of the drafting process.

Directions: Review your revised draft. Then circle each expectation that your article meets. If parts of your draft are inadequate, note what you will do to bring them up to expectations.

Meets Expectations Circled *"I did this . . . "*	Purpose *" . . . because it . . . "*	Does Not Yet Meet Expectations Notes to Improve *Explain what you need to do now*
A complex issue is organized well and presented clearly.	Increases reading speed and ease	
I changed general words to be more specific.	Increases reader interest and understanding	
I included quantitative details.	Provides context and a sense of proportion or scope to the issue	
I included qualitative details.	Builds reader interest in the issue, the community, the sources, and/or the stakeholders	
I eliminated unnecessary repeated words within paragraphs.	Increases reading speed and limits boredom	
I used short paragraphs of 1–3 sentences.	Increases reading speed and ease	
I included full and/or partial quotes.	Provides evidence and brings source opinions to life	
I attributed information to credible sources.	Makes it clear who provided information	
I used commas, periods, and quotation marks properly.	Helps sentences and paragraphs make sense	
There are no spelling errors.	Eliminates distractions	

Section A. 5, Table A.4: Instructor Notes on Student Writing (Chapter 8)

Instructors can provide formative feedback for students as part of the revision process. This feedback can align with adopted language arts standards. We reference the Career and College Readiness Anchor Standards in this table.

Instructor Notes

Meets Expectations Circled	Does Not Meet Expectations Notes to Improve
A complex issue is organized well and presented clearly. CCSS.ELA-LITERACY.CCRA.W.2	
Specific word choice provides clarity and increases reader interest. CCSS.ELA-LITERACY.CCRA.W.4 CCSS.ELA-LITERACY.CCRA.L.1	
Quantitative details and/or statistics help provide context and a sense of proportion or scope to the issue. CCSS.ELA-LITERACY.CCRA.W.2	
Qualitative details build a reader's interest in the issue, the community, the sources, and/or the stake-holders. CCSS.ELA-LITERACY.CCRA.W.3	
There are few unnecessary repeated words that slow the reader down or bore them. CCSS.ELA-LITERACY.CCRA.W.4 CCSS.ELA-LITERACY.CCRA.L.3	
Short paragraphs of 1–3 sentences make the text easy to read quickly. CCSS.ELA-LITERACY.CCRA.W.4 CCSS.ELA-LITERACY.CCRA.L.1 CCSS.ELA-LITERACY.CCRA.L.3	
Full and/or partial quotes are correctly attributed and provide evidence, bringing source viewpoints to life. CCSS.ELA-LITERACY.CCRA.W.2	
Information is attributed to credible sources so it's clear who provided it. CCSS.ELA-LITERACY.CCRA.W.2	
Commas, periods, quotation marks, and other appropriate punctuation are used well to organize sentences. CCSS.ELA-LITERACY.CCRA.L.2	

continues

Meets Expectations Circled	Does Not Meet Expectations Notes to Improve
There are no spelling errors to distract a reader. CCSS.ELA-LITERACY.CCRA.L.2	
Compare early and later drafts. Writing shows evidence of being more effective after revision. CCSS.ELA-LITERACY.CCRA.W.5 CCSS.ELA-LITERACY.CCRA.W.10	

Section A.6, Table A.5: Self and Peer Evaluation of Group Performance (Chapter 9)

Students can evaluate their own collaborative experience during or after the project.

Directions: Evaluate each group member, including yourself, with comments and points.

	My Name:	Name:	Name:	Name:
Collaboration *When our group was collaborating, this person:* **3** Listened to other's ideas. Contributed ideas and built on contributions of others. **2** Listened fairly well but may have interrupted at times. Rarely deepened the discussion. **1** Was overbearing. Interrupted. Didn't allow discussion of ideas other than own or did not listen or did not contribute.				
Participation *The way this person participated throughout the project was:* **4** Showed leadership at some point (describe it please)				

3 Contributed ideas. Actively spoke up. Brainstormed. **2** Contributed some ideas but was mainly passive. **1** Did nothing.				
Commitment *This person:* **3** Did all of what they committed to do. **2** Did some of what they committed to do. **1** Did nothing.				
Total points (Out of 10)				
Attendance How many class sessions were missed during the project? If they had absences, did this person take responsibility for their share of group work?				

Overall Work Contribution
What percentage of the work do you think was contributed by each person?
    Consider the scope of work to be helping research facts and find sources, helping interview, helping discuss and decide how the article should be written and revised, and helping to write, edit, revise multiple drafts.
    Write a percentage for each person in your group. When added up, the columns should equal 100%.
	%	%	%	%

Other observations:

Section A.7, Table A.6: Example of Summative Writing Assessment (Chapter 9)

A self-contained, postproject summative assessment may require students to view a brief interview, read a short transcript, and organize and write an informative article.

Journalistic Learning Summative Writing Assessment

Task Directions: Cassandra Fleckenstein was interviewed about her job as a wildland firefighter mentor in Vale, Oregon. Watch and listen to the video excerpt, taking notes on a piece of paper. Read the transcript. Then write a short informative article about what it takes to become a wildland firefighter out of high school. Use information from both the video and the transcript. Include qualitative details (descriptions) and quantitative details (numbers) in your article. Be accurate and avoid plagiarism.

LEVEL 4 Proficient	Integration of Information from Multiple Sources	Quantitative Details	Qualitative Details	Accuracy of Oral Information	Avoids plagiarism
What makes it proficient?	Cohesively integrates multiple details from both sources in an organized way. *e.g., weaves together related material from the two sources*	Provides *specific* quantitative details from *both* sources. *e.g., from video: "90 days," "600 feet," "16 hours a day," "14 days straight," "100 to 110 degrees"* *e.g., from transcript: "I'm only taking in 28," "six months of general work experience," "zero work experience"*	Provides *multiple specific* details observed visually in video. *e.g., clothes, appearance or setting: "wearing a firefighter's t-shirt," "sitting near a geographic map," "piercings"*	Accurately uses *specific* oral information *multiple* times. *e.g., directly quotes video more than once*	Uses direct quotes *and* paraphrases information, with proper attribution. *Note: Since only one person has been interviewed, it is expected the writer will acknowledge the interviewee's first and last name one time. After that, referring to the source by last name only (or even first name) or by a pronoun is satisfactory.*
Score	4	4	4	4	4

LEVEL 3 Sufficient	Integration of Information from Multiple Sources	Quantitative Details	Qualitative Details	Accuracy of Oral Information	Avoids plagiarism
What makes it sufficient? What more is needed?	Uses information from both sources in an organized but nonintegrated way. *e.g., "stacks" details from the video on top of details from the transcript*	Provides *specific* quantitative details from just *one* source.	Provides *only one* specific detail observed visually from the video source.	Accurately uses oral information but only in a general way, by paraphrasing or summarizing.	Uses proper attribution but does not use any direct quotes from either source.
Score	3	3	3	3	3

LEVEL 2 Emergent	Integration of Information from Multiple Sources	Quantitative Details	Qualitative Details	Accuracy of Oral Information	Avoids plagiarism
What makes it emergent? What more is needed?	Uses information from two sources without attention to organization. *e.g., Details seem to be randomly presented, such as in a list*	Provides general quantitative details rather than specific. *e.g., hot weather, instead of "110 degrees;" long time instead of "14 days straight"*	Provides one or more *general* visual details from video. *e.g., "indoors," "shirt," "map"*	Inaccurately uses oral information. *e.g., misquotes or mis-paraphrases material from video*	Does not give attribution anywhere in the article. *e.g., uses quotation marks for direct quotes but without identification, or paraphrases information without identifying source*
Score	2	2	2	2	2

continues

LEVEL 1 Ineffective	Integration of Information from Multiple Sources	Quantitative Details	Qualitative Details	Accuracy of Oral Information	Avoids plagiarism
What makes it ineffective?	Only uses information from one source.	Does not include quantitative details.	Does not include visual details from the video.	Does not use video material.	Uses exact material from either source without quote marks or attribution (plagiarizing).
Score	1	1	1	1	1

Comments:

Standards Assessed:

CCSS.ELA-LITERACY.CCRA.SL.2—Integrate and evaluate information presented in diverse media and formats, including visually, quantitatively, and orally.

CCSS.ELA-LITERACY.CCRA.W.8—Gather relevant information from multiple print and digital sources, assess the credibility and accuracy of each source, and integrate the information while avoiding plagiarism.

Section A.8, Figure A.2: Example of Student Feedback Survey (Chapter 9)

Students can provide feedback to the instructor after their journalistic learning project.

Student Evaluation of Journalistic Learning Unit

Directions: Please answer the questions based on your memory and experience. (Scale: 1 = lowest, 4 = highest)

Journalism/Media Understanding

1. Before this unit, my understanding of journalism & media was:
   ___ poor   ___ fair   ___ excellent
2. Now, my understanding of journalism & media is:
   ___ poor   ___ fair   ___ excellent

Journalism Ethics

3. Before this unit, I could describe some of the ethical rules that guide journalism: ___ yes   ___ no
4. Now, I can describe some of the ethical rules that guide journalism: ___ yes   ___ no

Fact-checking

5. Before this unit, my confidence about checking the credibility of online information was: ___ 1   ___ 2   ___ 3   ___ 4
6. Now, my confidence about checking the credibility of online information is: ___ 1   ___ 2   ___ 3   ___ 4

Spotting Bias

7. Before this unit, I could find evidence of bias in informative articles: ___ 1   ___ 2   ___ 3   ___ 4
8. Now, I can find evidence of bias in informative articles:
   ___ 1   ___ 2   ___ 3   ___ 4

Communicating with Community Members

9. Before this unit, my confidence in writing a professional email to a community member was: ___ 1   ___ 2   ___ 3   ___ 4
10. Now, my confidence in writing a professional email to a community member is: ___ 1   ___ 2   ___ 3   ___ 4

Interviewing

11. Before this unit, my confidence in developing quality interview questions was: ___ 1 ___ 2 ___ 3 ___ 4

12. Now, my confidence in developing quality interview questions is: ___ 1 ___ 2 ___ 3 ___ 4

Informative Writing

13. Before this unit, I felt my ability to write informatively was: ___ 1 ___ 2 ___ 3 ___ 4

14. Now, I feel my ability to write informatively is: ___ 1 ___ 2 ___ 3 ___ 4

Overall Experience of Unit

15. I feel like I learned skills that will be valuable for my future: ___ 1 ___ 2 ___ 3 ___ 4

16. I liked the way the lessons were organized: ___ 1 ___ 2 ___ 3 ___ 4

17. I'm happy with how the article I worked on turned out: ___ 1 ___ 2 ___ 3 ___ 4

18. I wish I could have worked by myself on this project: ___ yes ___ no

More of/Less of

19. In this unit, I would have liked more of:	20. In this unit, I would have liked less of:

Easy/Hard

21. One thing that was easier than I thought it would be at first was:	22. One thing that was harder than I thought it would be at first was:

Recommendation

23. Should this unit be taught to next year's students?

     ___ yes   ___ no

24. Please share why you answered the way you did:

Section A.9: Scholastic Journalism Resources (Chapter 9)

In addition to resources on the Journalistic Learning Initiative website, (https://journalisticlearning.org) a lot of support exists to help you learn how to start and advise a scholastic journalism program at your school, if you are interested in doing so.

Each of the national organizations below is dedicated to helping student journalists, advisers, and school publications thrive, and they are especially adept at providing beginning advisers with resources. One of us (Melissa) leaned on these organizations between 2009–2015 after she founded an online journalism class at Foothill Technology High School in Ventura, California. Your state or region also may have a robust journalism education organization.

Columbia Scholastic Press Association: The association was founded in 1925 at Columbia University in New York City. It supports seconday student editors and faculty advisers who produce student newspapers, magazines, yearbooks, and online media. CSPA hosts an annual fall conference at the university, as well as a spring convention and a summer intensive learning workshop for students and instructors. It recognizes student work in print or digital mediums through the Crown Awards and Circle Awards. The organization also honors advisers, including naming the National High School Journalism Teacher of the Year, and provides publication critiques that analyze strengths and weaknesses. Website: cspa.columbia.edu/

Journalism Education Association (JEA): The association was founded in 1924 and provides resources and educational opportunities to secondary journalism advisers. Headquartered in Manhattan, Kansas, the nonprofit offers training at annual fall and spring conventions around the country. It hosts a summer advisers' institute and offers national certification for teaching high school journalism. The JEA listserv offers a way for advisers to post questions and receive immediate answers from other advisers throughout the year. A mentoring program pairs veteran advisers with beginners. JEA publishes the quarterly magazine *Communication: Journalism Education Today*. Website: http://jea.org/wp/

National Scholastic Press Association: Founded in 1921, the association offers memberships for middle school, junior high, and high school publications. The nonprofit cohosts with JEA annual fall and spring conventions where students and advisers can develop their understanding and skills or take part in on-site competitions. NSPA offers a critique service and one-hour consultations. The organization honors top publications with the Pacemaker Award and the NSPA Hall of Fame and presents individual student awards across a range of categories. In 2022, NSPA inducted 1,300 students into its honor roll. Website: https://studentpress.org/nspa/

Student Press Law Center (SPLC): The national center was founded in 1974 as a nonpartisan nonprofit that supports journalism advisers and students by defending their First Amendment rights. Based in Washington, D.C., the SPLC runs a legal hotline, cultivates a nationwide attorney referral network, develops educational materials, and offers training and classroom visits across the country. The center also supports New Voices, a student-powered grassroots movement of student activists who are working to protect and increase student press freedom at the state level. Website: https://splc.org/

APPENDIX B

Professional Article

Note: The following professional news feature is useful as a mentor text for students to examine multiple times as they work on components of their project. The article provides a strong model of quotes, qualitative and quantitative details, balanced sources, a lede, a closing, journalistic paragraphs, AP style, and past–present–future organization.

Starlings in Oregon are an invasive pest to some, a fascinating species facing "bio bigotry" to others

BY MEGAN BANTA, *THE REGISTER-GUARD*

As employees at Short Mountain Landfill maneuver heavy machinery to compact trash, a throng of birds lifts and swarms before settling back down on the garbage.

The birds aren't seagulls, ravens, crows, or magpies—all of which are common at landfills.

They're European starlings.

An invasive species, starlings closely resemble blackbirds and often draw the ire of many birders, farmers and others because they can pose a threat to native bird species and crops. Invasive species are living organisms that are not native to an ecosystem and cause harm.

On farms, starlings are most noticeable among the pest birds, said Jenifer Cruikshank, who works for the Oregon State University Extension Service focusing on dairy farms

"There's just so many of them, and they're kind of voracious eaters," she said.

Starlings also have some beneficial qualities, though, said Dan Gleason, a former University of Oregon ornithology professor and owner of Wild Birds Unlimited in Eugene, such as the ability to eat some invasive insects.

People can do things to discourage starlings from coming back if they see them, said Gleason and Rick Boatner, invasive species coordinator for the Oregon Department of Fish and Wildlife.

The species is so well-established, Boatner said, that any efforts to drive them out might work temporarily but aren't likely to be permanent.

Introduction to U.S., Oregon

European starlings, as the descriptor in their name would suggest, did not originate in the United States.

While starlings look a lot like and often flock with blackbirds, there are ways to tell them apart. Both species have iridescent plumage, but starlings have a dark upper wing and pale underwing. During mating season, they also have a bright yellow bill.

They were introduced to Central Park from Europe in the late 1800s. The goal at the time, Gleason said, was to bring over every bird mentioned in Shakespeare's plays.

It took a couple tries for the birds to survive—starlings aren't forest birds, Gleason said. But starlings started flourishing after being released on Long Island, where it was urbanized enough for them to nest.

The state defines starlings as predatory animals and invasive and doesn't provide protection for the species like it does for native birds.

By the 1960s, the species was common in Oregon, Gleason said, and they have become numerous because "we've made good habitat" for them.

And where they go, they often drive other birds out of their nests to use as their own home.

Starlings are assertive, said Barbara Gleason, who runs Wild Birds Unlimited along with her husband.

Dan Gleason goes a step further, describing them as "a little aggressive." They can even drive a wood duck out of its nest, he said.

Damage to fields, other crops

They affect animals beyond other bird species, too.

On feed lots, Boatner, said, they'll eat food that's supposed to go to pigs and cows.

Cruickshank, who holds a doctorate in dairy science, works with dairy producers of all sizes and said starlings are a "major problem" on dairy farms and other farms with livestock.

Most dairy farmers are feeding hundreds and hundreds of cows, she said, and will store food in open bays so it's accessible. That also leaves it open to pest birds, including starlings, she said.

The birds will pick grain out of mixed food meant to cover all of a cow's nutritional needs, she said, and they mostly deplete spots near the entry of feed barns.

"What you'll get is the cows that end up in those more greatly depleted spots in the feed bunk are going to be your cows who are lower in the pecking order," Cruikshank said.

They also do damage on grass fields, Boatner said.

Starlings have a long beak and can pull up and eat planted seeds, hindering crop production.

They generally don't enjoy seeds, Dan Gleason said, but they do like to eat apples, blueberries, cherries, strawberries, figs, and many other cultivated fruits.

They'll take little bites out of individual cherries, Cruikshank added, and generally cause issues for fruit producers.

Starlings also are numerous in the United States—based on population counts, there are more in the U.S. now than there are in Europe.

They're especially abundant in urban areas.

"They habitat around people really well," Boatner said. "They've learned really well to take advantage of humans."

Yet many humans find them an annoyance.

Little things make them "not as negative"

For some people, that's simply bias toward starlings as a non-native species, Dan Gleason said.

He called this attitude "bio bigotry" and said it can mean people don't really take the time to look at a species because of prejudice.

Dan Gleason doesn't want to see starlings proliferate, but they do some things that are beneficial.

For example, they can push their beak down in a hole and push deep enough to get larvae of crane flies that native birds miss, and they eat other agricultural pests, many of which also aren't native.

They're pretty in their own way, Barbara Gleason said, and it's often beautiful when they fly in swooping, intricately coordinated patterns through the sky. That pattern, known as a murmuration, is more common in Europe, and scientists believe the birds use it as protection from predators.

They're also good mimics, Dan Gleason said. If you hear a duck up a tree or a hawk screech without seeing one in the sky, it could be a starling.

Little things, he said, make them not as negative, and there are plenty of fascinating things about starlings.

"As a birder, you don't really want to see them around," he said. "As a biologist, I find them fascinating."

Biologists like Dan Gleason know so much about starlings—and, often by extension, other birds—because they're used heavily in research. You don't need a permit to take starlings from the wild or research on them like you do for native birds.

Take away their food source and they'll leave

For those who do see starlings as pests, though, there are ways to get rid of them.

People can do "just about anything" to starlings, including shooting and trapping them, if they don't violate a city or county ordinance, Boatner said.

The Gleasons recommend less drastic measures, though.

People can drive them away with CDs or foil tins or noise cannons, they said, but the birds typically figure out the distractions or loud noises won't hurt them and come back.

The best thing to do, Dan Gleason said, is to take away their food source.

That's going to be hard somewhere like the landfill, he said, where they're likely gathering because of an abundance of insects and other invertebrates.

The county tries to manage starlings and other bird populations at the landfill by restricting how much area is being used to compact trash, spokeswoman Devon Ashbridge said.

"By reducing the footprint of the open cell, we make it a less attractive location for the starlings," she said.

The landfill supervisor implemented the technique a few years ago, she said, and it has helped.

People can help the landfill manage starlings by reducing the amount of food waste they throw out, Ashbridge added.

Food makes up about 18% of what an average resident throws away and is the single largest category in the county's waste stream, said Angie Marzano, a waste reduction specialist for the county.

Around 20 to 30% of what people throw away could have been eaten, she said, and part of the county's effort to reduce food waste is "just trying to teach residents to eat the food that they buy."

"One of the single greatest things you can do is just eating the expensive, organic food that you buy," Marzano said.

People who live in a house in Eugene can put any food waste they do generate into their yard debris container, she said, and those who live in apartments could try reaching out to a neighbor or a participating restaurant nearby.

It doesn't take a lot of effort, Marzano added, but has many benefits.

In the case of bird feeders, it's a little easier to deter starlings, Barbara Gleason said. She recommends people use a suet feeder and put it in a cage so the starlings can't reach in.

There are "all sorts of bird feeder designs" that can discourage starlings, Boatner said.

Farmers, landfill operators and others dealing with large populations can contact a wildlife control agent with the U.S. Department of Agriculture. There's an office of the department's wildlife services program in Portland.

APPENDIX C

Student Article

Note: *The following was written by Leila Goodwin, an 11th-grade student in Patrick McDonald's English class at Oregon City High School in Oregon City, Oregon. It was published June 16, 2022, in* The Elevator, *a class online newspaper, the culmination of a journalistic learning project. It is reprinted verbatim here. The author had no previous journalism experience.*

Portland's housing supply problem: Will the shortage have a solution?

BY LEILA GOODWIN

Portland, Oregon is a beautiful metropolitan area surrounded by lush forests, snowy mountains, and wide rivers. For outdoor enthusiasts, the city is only a short drive from activities such as skiing, biking, and river rafting, as well as only an hour and a half from the beach.

With all this natural beauty, it's no surprise that the city is such an attractive place to live. In the last 20 years, Oregon's population has increased by 22.2% (beating the national average by around 5%), and the city of Portland itself has grown even faster.

However, along with this rapid population increase comes an increasing need for housing in and near the city, so that people can commute into the city to work. As this demand increases, consumers and policymakers alike have found themselves running into a major problem: restrictive urban growth boundaries that have caused Portland homes to skyrocket in value.

Dr. Gerard Mildner, a professor at PSU and expert in real estate finance, says that Portland's urban growth restrictions were developed as a response to other states' urban sprawl. "A lot of our land use laws were written in the 1970s . . . and the intent was to avoid the planning outcomes that happened in California," Dr. Mildner explains. "And so, we've had within the Portland Metro Area, on the Oregon side at least, a growth boundary. In other countries, you might call it a green belt, but basically the idea was to prevent urban area from expanding into the agricultural areas."

In theory, this "green belt" provides an environmental buffer between urban and rural areas by preventing large, sprawling suburbs that provide housing for upper middle class families at the expense of the forest and agricultural industries.

However, these well-intentioned land use policies have had unintended consequences: as the population increases, it reduces the amount of land per person in urban areas. According to Mildner, "since the boundary's been established, our metropolitan population has expanded by 80%, but our UGB—our urban growth boundary—has only expanded by 15%. And this is a chronic problem."

Urban expansion vs. agricultural preservation

In the 1970s, as Portland's population was beginning to grow more quickly, city planners were facing a dilemma: Portland's urban growth was beginning to expand out from city boundaries and into surrounding communities, prompting developers to take interest in land further from city center.

California, and other states before it, had allowed this development to take place without much regulation, blending urban and rural through dozens of miles of sprawling suburbs that surrounded their largest cities.

Instead of allowing this same kind of unchecked expansion in Oregon, Metro officials turned to northern European countries like the UK as an example of a more "sustainable" approach to urban growth. The result? Portland's unique "green belt."

"We have many, many parcels that are exclusively for farm use, or exclusively for forest use." Mildner asserts. "Once you go beyond the boundary, you can't really develop housing, insofar as it's kind of 'one house per farm' or, you know, 'one house per forested lot'." What's more, Mildner says, in the Willamette Valley, these parcels of land can't be split up any smaller than 50 acres. If that same amount of land was inside Portland's UGB, it could theoretically fit 400 houses.

Furthermore, Mildner argues, the state's requirements for Metro to provide enough land for housing are vague. Metro is required to zone enough land for a 20 year supply of housing. "The problem is that that's a really undefined concept," says Mildner, "because if you develop a density of, let's say, Brooklyn, New York, or Philadelphia, you could pack a lot of people into an acre of housing. On the other hand, if you build them at lower densities, like might be more typical of a place like Oregon City, you might need a lot more land. The decision of whether to expand the boundary is somewhat subjective, even though it's got this official '20 year land supply' in the regulation."

These policies mean that, while there is an abundance of land surrounding Portland, there is a shortage of housing.

According to Mildner, this isn't necessarily unique to Portland. "The reason why San Francisco and Los Angeles have higher housing prices is because their land costs are higher. You're trying to squeeze more and more people into a given metro area."

For cities like San Francisco that don't have enough land to continue expanding their metro area to keep up with population growth, this price increase is unavoidable. For Portland, it's the price residents pay to keep their community green.

Zoning and infrastructure changes could make building new housing easier

While expanding the urban growth boundary is one possible solution to the housing supply problem, there are other policies Metro could—or already did—attempt to rework to better fit current population needs.

One of these potential areas for change are zoning laws. According to Cornell's law dictionary, a zoning law is "a municipal law that outlines permitted uses for various sections of land." When talking about residential housing, zoning laws can outline how tall buildings can be, and even how many families can live in them.

Dr. Mildner recognizes that Metro is already working to adjust its zoning laws. "We've done some good things, at the state level, to reform single-family zoning," he remarks. "Cities all across the region are now adjusting their zoning policies to allow for accessory dwelling units and duplexes in a lot of neighborhoods that have previously been single-family homes."

However, Mildner warns that these changes won't be as effective as planners hope. He notices that Oregon housing production, which slowed during the 2008 recession, has still not returned to the same level it was at in the 1990s.

One cause of this ineffectiveness, according to Mildner, are laws known as inclusionary zoning laws—laws that attempt to account for the difficulties faced by low-income families in paying a monthly rent. These laws make developers and investors more hesitant to commit to building new housing, as they often take losses from stipulations such as mandated rent reductions.

Another policy that might lower housing prices is the construction of more roads. When access to rural areas is facilitated by an increase in roadways, it incentivizes developers to construct housing along those roads, and allows them to do so more quickly and easily.

Unfortunately, increasing road construction is often controversial. More roads often mean less land for forest and agriculture, not to mention an increase in cars on the road, all of which often concerns environmentalists.

Mildner, however, believes these concerns are less pressing than Portland's housing shortage. "Compounding that issue is global warming, but we also have the potential for cars which are much less polluting, if not electric, so to me, that whole issue is a red herring. We should be building more roads to facilitate housing construction."

Pandemic solutions: short-term success

Portland's officials recognize that rising prices have contributed to financial insecurity and rising rates of homelessness. According to Jordan Mulvihill, a graduate student in the Master of Real Estate Department and a fellow with the Oregon Association of Realtors at PSU, "In October 2015, Portland City Council declared a state of emergency to help address the city's growing homeless and housing affordability crisis."

These issues have only gotten worse since 2015, as the world has had to grapple with the lasting effects of the COVID-19 pandemic.

Oregon's legislature has come up with a number of solutions, the first of which was the distribution of the 204 million dollars granted in Federal Emergency Rental Assistance under the 2020 CARES Act.

Dan March, a Multi-Family Northwest student fellow, writes, "In December 2020, Oregon passed House Bill 4401 which arranged $150 million to be distributed by Oregon Housing and Community Services ('OHCS') through the Landlord Compensation Fund ('LCF')." This original distribution was followed by subsequent extensions and distributions, eventually leading to a "new phase of rental assistance funding" that will foreseeably continue to use federal rent assistance to subsidize rents until 2025.

Federal money, however, is not the only source of relief for renters. Oregon's state legislature has also began developing housing projects to provide low cost apartments for those most in danger of being unable to afford Portland's high cost of living.

One of these, Project Turnkey, "uses grant money to acquire hotels and motels to use as emergency housing during the pandemic, with intentions to convert them into a permanent supply of transitional, supportive, and affordable housing units . . . Project Turnkey was able to acquire and convert 865 new housing units in Oregon, at the average cost of $87,700 per unit. That's over 60% less [than] the average cost of a new affordable housing unit," Mulvihill says.

According to Nate Grein, another graduate student in the MRED, two other programs, the Portland Housing Bond and Metro Housing Bond, are, "partly responsible for Portland seeing one of the largest per-capita investments in affordable housing in the entire U.S."

Gen Z: grew up in Portland, but can't afford to live here

As Portland families grow older, many young people are looking to rent their first apartment or other living space. Unfortunately, homeownership and renting in Portland have changed since their parents bought homes 20 years ago. Despite recent political efforts to increase renter's assistance, the government can only afford subsidize the market for the short-term.

According to rentdata.org, the rent for a studio apartment in the Clackamas County Metro is almost $500 above Oregon's "fair market rent," a number determined by the Department of Housing and Urban Development to determine the scope of government aid for federally assisted housing. And as the rental you're looking at gains extra bedrooms, or amenities, the gap only widens.

These high rents aren't realistic for someone working on or near minimum wage. First time renters who are looking to live near where they work in Portland might be in for a shock, especially as rising interest rates, ushered in by federal increases this spring, are already affecting the market. The reality is that Portland may be turning into a city whose rental rates can't accommodate those with less established careers, or those who are in a less stable financial situation.

This problem originated, Jordan Mulvihill writes, when single-room occupancies, or SROs, began to be converted from rentable residential dwellings into, "offices, luxury condos, or tourists' hotels."

"Housing nonprofit Northwest Pilot Project found that from 1978 to 2015, Downtown lost nearly 40% of its rentals (about 2,000 units) that were affordable to minimum wage earners. Many of these units were SROs," Mulvihill said.

This incredible reduction in the amount of viable housing for low-earners, like young adults just out of high school or college, in Portland has meant that new renters might have to start looking elsewhere to rent their first apartment or buy their first homes.

"If we stay with the policies we're on, I think the outcome that's most likely for Portland is what I sometimes call the Santa Barbara solution," Mildner said. "If you're a young person growing up in Santa Barbara, and you don't have, you know, a rich daddy, and you don't have a great job, you're not gonna live in Santa Barbara. You're gonna move to the places where job opportunities are more plentiful, and housing is more affordable."

For Gen Z, this could mean moving to a surrounding community like Beaverton, Tualatin, Gresham, or Oregon City. It could also mean moving away from Portland entirely, and relocating to Salem, Eugene or even out of state entirely. As Portland's housing market becomes more competitive, Portlanders may have to ask themselves: Is living here really worth the cost?

REFERENCES

Abernathy, P. M. (2018). *The expanding news desert*. UNC School of Media and Journalism's Center for Innovation and Sustainability in Local Media. https://www.usnewsdeserts.com/reports/expanding-news-desert/

Amazeen, M. A., & Wojdynski, B. W. (2019). Reducing native advertising deception: Revisiting the antecedents and consequences of persuasion knowledge in digital news contexts. *Mass Communication and Society, 22*(2), 222–247. https://doi.org/10.1080/15205436.2018.1530792

APM Research Lab, & The McCourtney Institute for Democracy. (2022). *Mood of the Nation poll: How Americans think schools should teach the topics of slavery & race, evolution, and sexual education*. https://static1.squarespace.com/static/5c9542c8840b163998cf4804/t/62bdc6c951ebb35a4aebccef/1656604362555/MOTN-APMResearchLab-Liberty%28June2022%29.pdf

Associated Press, The. (1960, January 29). U.S. bars a girl's plea for Russian pen pals. *The New York Times*, A4.

Associated Press, The. (2019). *The Associated Press stylebook 2019: And briefing on media law*. The Associated Press.

Banta, M. (2021, April 17). Starlings in Oregon are an invasive pest to some, a fascinating species facing "bio bigotry" to others. *The Register-Guard*. https://www.registerguard.com/story/news/2021/04/17/starlings-oregon-non-native-invasive-murmuration/4566680001/

Banta, M. (2022, April 6). Eugene "bailing out Titanic with a teacup" helping people living in vehicles and addressing impacts. *The Register-Guard*. https://www.registerguard.com/story/news/homelessness/2022/04/06/oregon-homelessness-eugene-new-vehicle-parking-rules-impacts/65063370007/

Bell, S. (2010). Project-based learning for the 21st century: Skills for the future. *The Clearing House, 83*, 39–43. https://doi.org/10.1080/00098650903505415

Birnbauer, B. (2018). *The rise of nonprofit investigative journalism in the United States*. Routledge.

Block, M. K., & Strachan, S. L. (2019). The impact of external audience on second graders' writing quality. *Reading Horizons: A Journal of Literacy and Language Arts, 58*(2), 68–93. https://scholarworks.wmich.edu/reading_horizons/vol58/iss2/5

Breakstone, J., Smith, M., Wineburg, S., Rapaport, A., Carle, J., Garland, M., & Saavedra, A. (2021). Students' civic online reasoning: A national portrait. *Educational Researcher, 50*(8), 505–515. https://doi.org/10.3102/0013189X211017495

Brenan, M. (2020). *Americans remain distrustful of mass media*. Gallup. https://news
.gallup.com/poll/321116/americans-remain-distrustful-mass-media.aspx

Caulfield, M. (2019, June 19). SIFT (The four moves). *Hapgood*. https://hapgood
.us/2019/06/19/sift-the-four-moves/

Cooper, A. (2019, May 11). *FDA warns chemicals from sunscreen enter your bloodstream
after one day*. Moms. https://www.moms.com/chemicals-from-sunscreen-enter
-bloodstream-fda-warns/

Duke, N. K. (2016). Project-based instruction: A great match for informational texts.
American Educator, 40(3), 4–11; 42.

Eells, J. (2019). Billie Eilish and the triumph of the weird. *Variety*. https://www
.rollingstone.com/music/music-features/billie-eilish-cover-story-triumph
-weird-863603/

Federal Trade Commission. (2015). Enforcement policy statement on deceptively formatted advertisements. https://www.ftc.gov/system/files/documents/public_sta
tements/896923/151222deceptiveenforcement.pdf

Freire, P. (2018). *Pedagogy of the oppressed* (50th anniversary edition). Bloomsbury
Academic.

Garcia, A. (2021, December 6). A new, more restrictive 'critical race theory' law now in
effect for Texas schools. *The Houston Chronicle*. https://www.chron.com/politics/
article/Texas-critical-race-theory-law-schools-16678700.php

Glaser, A. (2017, January 22). *In his first full day in office, President Trump declared war on
the media*. Vox. https://www.vox.com/2017/1/22/14350406/president-trump-cia
-war-media-speech

Godfrey, E. (2021). What we lost when Gannett came to town. *The Atlantic*. https://
www.theatlantic.com/politics/archive/2021/10/gannett-local-newspaper-hawk
-eye-iowa/619847/

Goodwin, Leila. (2022). Portland's housing supply problem: Will the shortage have
a solution? *The Elevator*. https://sites.google.com/orecity.k12.or.us/theelevator/
affordable-housing?

Gramlich, J. (2019). *Young Americans are less trusting of other people–and key institutions–than their elders*. Pew Research Center. https://www.pewresearch.org/fact
-tank/2019/08/06/young-americans-are-less-trusting-of-other-people-and-key
-institutions-than-their-elders/

Groen, M. (2013). Teaching, learning, and emerging national identity in the Antebel-
lum South. *American Educational History Journal, 40*(1), 21–35.

Guldin, R., Madison, E., & Anderson, R. (2021). Writing for social justice: Journalistic
strategies for catalyzing agentic engagement among Latinx middle school students through media education. *Journal of Media Literacy Education, 13*(2), 71–85.
https://doi.org/10.23860/JMLE-2021-13-2-6

Hanson, G. (2002). Learning journalism ethics: The classroom versus the real
world. *Journal of Mass Media Ethics, 17*(3), 235–247. https://doi.org/10.1207/
S15327728JMME1703_05

Head, A. J., Fister, B., & MacMillan, M. (2020). *Information literacy in the age of algorithms: Student experiences with news and information, and the need for change*. Proj-

ect Information Literacy. https://projectinfolit.org/pubs/algorithm-study/
pil_algorithm-study_2020-01-15.pdf

Healy, J. (2014, September 23). In Colorado, a student counterprotest to an anti-protest curriculum. *The New York Times.* https://www.nytimes.com/2014/09/24/us/in-colorado-a-student-counterprotest-to-an-anti-protest-curriculum.html

Hechinger, F. M. (1984, January 3). Censorship rises in the nation's public schools. *The New York Times,* C7.

Hiestand, M. (n.d.). *Avoid legal pitfalls in changing names of sources.* National Student Press Association. https://studentpress.org/nspa/avoid-legal-pitfalls-in-changing-names-of-sources/

Hobbs, R. (2020). *Mind over media: Propaganda education for a digital age.* Norton.

Huss, N. (2022, April 7). *How many websites are there in the world?* Siteefy. https://siteefy.com/how-many-websites-are-there/

Ifill, G. (2013, May 20). *Remarks* [Address]. Wake Forest University commencement, Winston-Salem, NC, United States. https://commencement.news.wfu.edu/2010s/c2013/2013-speaker-gwen-ifill/

Kersten, S. (2017). Becoming nonfiction authors: Engaging in science inquiry. *The Reading Teacher, 71*(1), 33–41. https://www.jstor.org/stable/26632505

Kownslar, A. O. (2019). *The great Texas social studies textbook war of 1961–1962.* Texas A&M University Press.

LaMotte, S. (2019, May 6). *Sunscreen enters bloodstream after just one day of use, study says.* CNN. https://www.cnn.com/2019/05/06/health/sunscreen-bloodstream-fda-study

Lanier, L. (2019, May 22). "Mario Kart Tour" beta locks powerful "rare" characters behind paywall. *Variety.* https://variety.com/2019/gaming/news/mario-kart-tour-monetization-beta-1203223369/

Laufer, P. (2020). *Classroom 15: How the Hoover FBI censored the dreams of innocent Oregon fourth graders.* Anthem Press.

Madison, E. (2015). *Newsworthy: Cultivating critical thinkers, readers, and writers in language arts classrooms.* Teachers College Press.

Madison, E., Anderson, R., & Bousselot, T. (2019). Self-determined to write: leveraging interest, collaboration, and self-direction through a journalistic approach. *Reading & Writing Quarterly, 35*(5), 473–495. https://doi.org/10.1080/10573569.2019.1579127

Mazzei, P. (2022, March 28). DeSantis signs Florida bill that opponents call 'don't say gay'. *New York Times,* A17. https://www.nytimes.com/2022/03/28/us/desantis-florida-dont-say-gay-bill.html

McLuhan, M. (1964). *Understanding media.* McGraw-Hill.

Mehan, H. (1979). *Learning lessons: Social organization in the classroom.* Harvard University Press.

Method. (n.d). T Brand. Retrieved February 25, 2020, from https://web.archive.org/web/20220515003406/https://www.tbrandstudio.com/method/

Mickanen, D. (2021, March 19). *Sedona Prince's viral TikTok shows the NCAA had enough space for an equal weight room.* NBC Sports. https://www.nbcsports.com/

northwest/oregon-ducks/sedona-princes-viral-tiktok-shows-ncaa-had-enough
-space-equal-weight-room

Modern Language Association. (2020). Should media in reference to mass media be treated as a singular or plural noun? *MLA Style Center.* https://style.mla.org/media-singular-or-plural/

National Center for Education Statistics. (2012). *The nation's report card: Writing 2011* (NCES 2012–470). U.S. Department of Education, Institute of Education Sciences. https://nces.ed.gov/nationsreportcard/pubs/main2011/2012470.aspx

National Council of Teachers of English. (2022). *Media education in English language arts.* https://ncte.org/statement/media_education/

National Governors Association Center for Best Practices & Council of Chief State School Officers. (2010). Common Core State Standards for English language arts and literacy in history/social studies, science, and technical subjects. Washington, DC: Authors.

Nolan, M. F. (2005). Orwell meets Nixon: When and why "the press" became "the media." *International Journal of Press/Politics, 10*(2), 69–84. https://doi.org/10.1177/1081180X05277630

Peterlin, L. J., & Peters, J. (2019). Teaching journalism ethics through "The Newsroom": An enhanced learning experience. *Journalism & Mass Communication Educator, 74*(1), 44–59. https://doi.org/10.1177/1077695818767230

Pew Research Center. (2021). *Newspaper fact sheet.* https://www.pewresearch.org/journalism/fact-sheet/newspapers/

Pronin, E., Lin, D. Y., & Ross, L. (2002). The bias blind spot: Perceptions of bias in self versus others. *Personality and Social Psychology Bulletin, 28*(3), 369–381. https://doi.org/10.1177/0146167202286008

Rideout, V., & Robb, M. B. (2019). *The Common Sense census: Media use by teens and tweens.* Common Sense Media. https://www.commonsensemedia.org/sites/default/files/research/report/2019-census-8-to-18-full-report-updated.pdf

Schulten, K. (2022). *Coming of age in 2020: Teenagers on the year that changed everything.* Norton.

Schulten, K. (2020). *Raising student voice: 35 ways to help students write better argument essays.* Norton.

Smith, D. (2019, September 7). "Enemy of the people": Trump's war on the media is a page from Nixon's playbook. *The Guardian.* https://www.theguardian.com/us-news/2019/sep/07/donald-trump-war-on-the-media-oppo-research

Society of Professional Journalists. (2014). *SPJ code of ethics.* https://www.spj.org/ethicscode.asp

Southern Poverty Law Center. (2018, January 18). *The miseducation of Dylan Roof* [Video]. YouTube. https://www.youtube.com/watch?v=qB6A45tA6mE

Stand for Children, & Survey USA. (2022). *National teacher survey uncovers right wing culture war's destructive impact on public education.* https://stand.org/wp-content/uploads/2022/06/Teacher-Survey_1221.pdf

Steinberg, A. (1997). *Real learning, real work: School-to-work as high school reform.* Routledge.

Swift, A. (2016). *Americans' trust in mass media sinks to new low.* Gallup. https://news
    .gallup.com/poll/195542/americans-trust-mass-media-sinks-new-low.aspx

Thier, D. (2019, May 23). Bad news: 'Mario Kart Tour' on mobile has nasty micro-
    transactions. *Forbes.* https://www.forbes.com/sites/davidthier/2019/05/23/bad
    -news-mario-kart-tour-on-mobile-has-nasty-microtransactions/

Van Syckle, K. (2021, May 6). How a fourth grader in 1960 inspired college students
    in 2019. *The New York Times,* A2. https://www.nytimes.com/2021/05/06/insider/
    class-russia-children.html

Virtue, E. E., & Hinnant-Crawford, B. N. (2019). "We're doing things that are mean-
    ingful": Student perspectives of project-based learning across the disciplines.
    The Interdisciplinary Journal of Problem-Based Learning, 13(2). https://doi.org/10
    .7771/1541-5015.1809

Walder, J. C., & Cleveland, A. D. (1971). The South's new segregation academies. *The Phi
    Delta Kappan, 53*(4), 234–235, 238–239. https://www.jstor.org/stable/20373159

Wineburg, S., & McGrew, S. (2017). *Lateral reading: Reading less and learning more when
    evaluating digital information.* Stanford History Education Group. http://dx.doi
    .org/10.2139/ssrn.3048994

INDEX

ABOUT THE AUTHORS

Ed Madison's multifaceted career in media and journalism began as a high school intern at the *Washington Post*-owned CBS television affiliate in Washington, D.C., during the height of Watergate. At age 22, CNN recruited him as a founding producer. Madison is an associate professor at the University of Oregon School of Journalism and Communication and a College of Education affiliated faculty member. His research centers on how journalistic learning methods can enhance overall student achievement. He is also a cofounder and executive director of the Journalistic Learning Initiative (JLI), a nonprofit committed to empowering student voice and academic success.

Melissa Wantz develops writing projects and supports teachers at the Journalistic Learning Initiative in Eugene, Oregon. As a middle and high school language arts teacher for two decades, she drew on her professional experience as a newspaper reporter to create curricula that sparked curiosity and built communications confidence in students. One of her highlights was founding the award-winning student news outlet at Foothill Technology High School in Ventura, California. That endeavor led to an invitation to serve on the advisory board of the Columbia Scholastic Press Association in New York and to present community-focused journalistic learning models nationally and abroad.

Dr. Rachel Guldin is an assistant professor of communication at Denison University. Her teaching and research examine issues of racism and capitalism through lenses of critical media literacy and critical political economy of communication. She received her PhD from the School of Journalism and Communication at the University of Oregon, where she researched how racism and capitalism can manifest in news literacy education. Before earning her doctorate, she taught English language arts and social studies as an elementary teacher in public schools. Guldin is proud to be the middle daughter of public school teachers.